THE
CELTIC DESIGN
BOOK

Aidan Meehan

With 900 illustrations

Aidan Meehan studied Celtic art in Ireland and Scotland and has spent the last four decades playing a leading role in the renaissance of this authentic tradition. He has given workshops, demonstrations and lectures in Europe and the USA, and more recently throughout the Pacific North West from his home base in Vancouver, B.C., Canada.

This omnibus edition first published in the United Kingdom in 2007 by Thames & Hudson Ltd, 181A High Holborn, London WC1V 7QX

Reprinted 2023

Originally published in the Celtic Design series as three separate volumes, *A Beginner's Manual*, *Knotwork* and *Illuminated Letters*

British Library Cataloguing-in-Publication Data
A catalogue record for this book is available from the British Library

ISBN 978-0-500-28674-6

Printed in China by Shenzhen Reliance Printing Co. Ltd

Be the first to know about our new releases, exclusive content and author events by visiting
thamesandhudson.com
thamesandhudsonusa.com
thamesandhudson.com.au

PART ONE

CELTIC DESIGN

❖

A BEGINNER'S MANUAL

CONTENTS

ERE for the first time is a manual of Celtic design for beginners which gives the form of construction of step patterns and key patterns based on the hitherto secret grid method of the scribes. This method is simple, a matter of joining the dots.

Almost as simple is the freehand construction of the spiral, given here along with a selection of treatments from early Celtic metalwork.

Compass work is also important to Celtic design, and here it is combined with the construction of letters, the decoration of which is suggested as an application.

TEP PATTERNS

Step patterns, found in the illuminated books, metal- and stonework, are very sim-ple, and illu-strate the in-telligibility of form that characterises Celtic pattern. Here are a few examples for you to repro-duce.

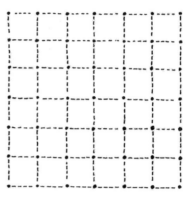

a. Six-square grid.

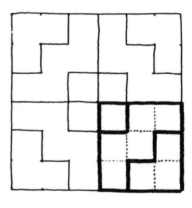

b. Same grid; each quarter is a three-square step pattern.

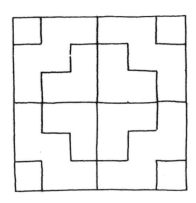

c. The quarters re-
arranged.

d. Same three-
square unit in
six-square grid.

Usually the
design is work-
ed out on a
simple square
grid of dots in
which repeats
of a smaller
unit may be
arranged in
different com-
binations as
here, a, b, c, d.
These patterns,
b, c, d, are based
on the smaller
repeat, b.

a. This one is made of four units, each one based on a four-square grid. Together the four units fill an eight-square.

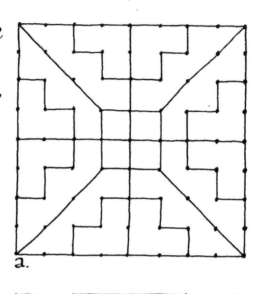

a.

b. If we change the order of the tiles, this is one result.

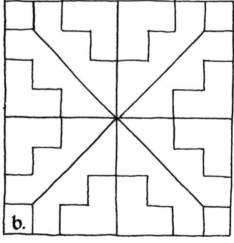

b.

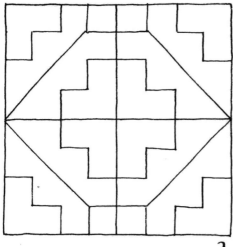

a.

On this page, the same eight-square grid has been used, and the quadrants are identical. Only their arrangement has been changed.

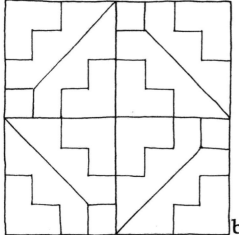

b.

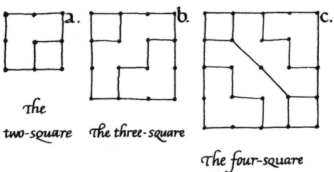

The
two-square   The three-square

The four-square

A GREAT many beautiful
overall patterns may be
produced by the tile met-
hod, as shown on previous pages.
The three-square, b, is used on
pages 10 and 11. The four-square,
c, is a variation of the tile unit
used in the patterns on page 12
and 13.

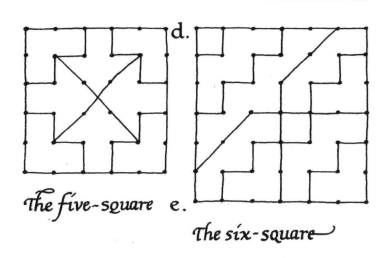

The five-square   d.

The six-square   e.

In these two we see the diagonal line used, as on previous
page, c, to tie-in points on the
grid otherwise floating free of
the step lines. A single square
might also have been used to connect the centre dots of fig. d.

ATTERNS are pleasing when they are reasonably well balanced. The two~square tile, a, below, is not balanced, yet four units make a very balanced pattern, b, that fills a four~square grid.

Three tiles will fit a six~square along each side, c, but the result is not a pattern. It is useful as a tile, though, and could be

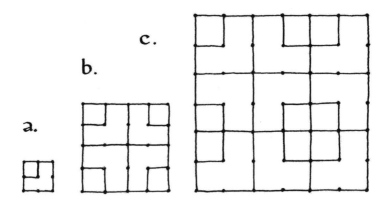

a.

b.

c.

arranged in each quarter of a twelve-square dot grid.

The pattern below is on an eight-square grid, d. Each quarter is the same design as that on the opposite page, b, used here as a tile. In the middle of the pattern, d, a further tile unit emerges. Compare this unit, e, with that at b. The respective modules are shown at f and a.

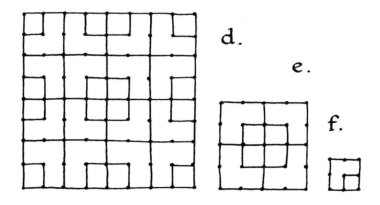

d.

e.

f.

N this page, the three ~ square tile, *a*, is expanded to fill a six~square and a twelve~square lay-out.

Four units combine to form the six~square, *b*. In turn, four of these make up the larger square, *c*. The centre four tiles in *fig.c* provide a further variation.

On page 19, a four~square tile: compare with pages 12, 13.

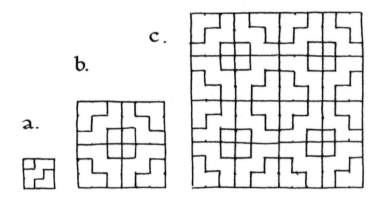

c.

b.

a.

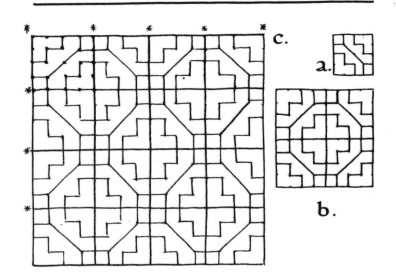

c.

a.

b.

N the manuscripts these step patterns are used as fillers, drawn freehand, or aided by a grid. To draw the grid for c, above, lay out the 4 x 4 squares in pencil, as indicated by asterisks. Then dot in the tile grid, as at top left, and ink in the lines, tile by tile.

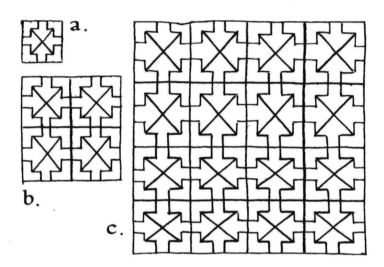

a.

b.

c.

METALWORK is another art in which the Celtic artists used step pattern, this one from the Lemanahan shrine, Ireland, 12th century. The design above appears as an enamel stud. It joins all the dots of a five-by-five square grid. Repeated in four and sixteen units, b, c.

THIS beauty is showcased in the Book of Lindisfarne, in a major piece of work, one of the exceptions, for step patterns are usually neglected. But the type of design you see here represents a mature tradition in its bloom, a widely practised art form. It has been sadly overlooked, a fact that is

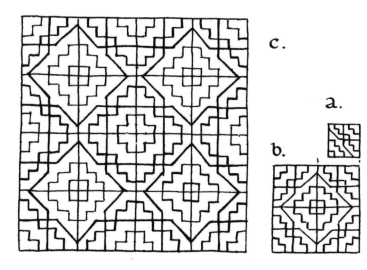

c.

a.

b.

---

brought out by a search through the
manuscripts.. there are few of any
great, and a lot of very little interest.
So the whole class is often overlooked, which is a pity. Master the step
patterns. They provide a key to the
metal smith's art of over-all grid
layout: this is the basis of Celtic
carpet-page design.

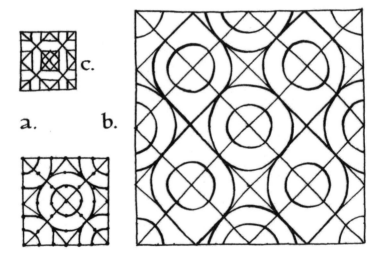

The pattern opposite, from the Book of Kells, uses circles instead of steps, but is developed from a grid, nevertheless, a,c.

Below, from the Book of Durrow, a combination of circle and step, derived from the six-square grid, b.

c.

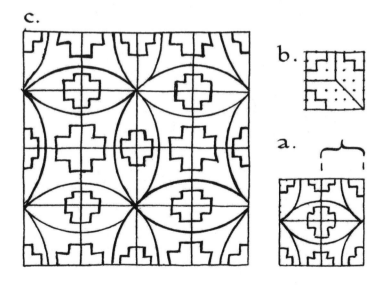

b.

a.

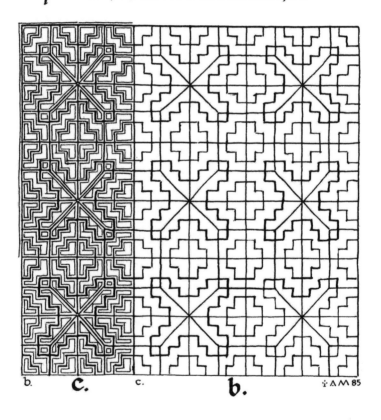

FIG. *b*, on previous page has dots to spare that may be joined by step lines, *a*, then repeated, *b*, and outlined, *c*.

a.

b.   **c.**   c.   **b.**   ✝ A M 85

KEY PATTERNS go well with other kinds of Celtic pattern. Here, borders of step pattern and plait work combine with the cross of key pattern.

S WITH STEP patterns and plaitwork, key patterns are easily made by join-the-dots. As in plaitwork, the lines are placed in such a way as to create paths.

Key patterns are found worldwide. Celtic key patterns are based on a particular system, developed from a ba~ sic square building block, Fig. 1, b. The basic key pattern starts out on a square grid, 7 spaces across and 7 down, enclosed by the sides of a square. This box and these dots define the

Fig. 1, α.

Fig. 1, b.

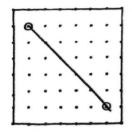

Fig. 2, a.

Fig. 2, b.

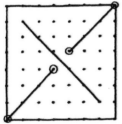

pattern.

In drawing the pat-
tern, the lines follow a
certain order. This is
called the stroke order,
as illustrated on this
and the following
pages, Fig. 2, a ~ j.

The diagonals should
be drawn first, Fig. 2,
a, b. The first diagonal
goes through the mid-
dle cell, but not the
corners, Fig. 2, a. The second cuts
through the corners, not the centre.
Fig. 2, b. Next draw the "arrow-
heads" on the ends of the first
diagonal, Fig. 2, c ~ f.

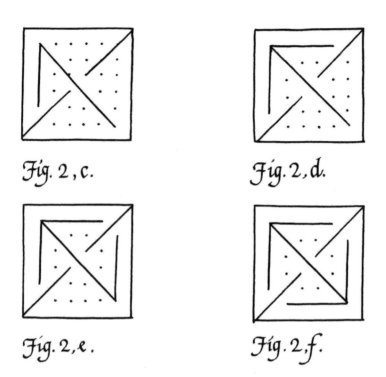

Fig. 2, c.

Fig. 2, d.

Fig. 2, e.

Fig. 2, f.

The arrow heads define the corners at each end of the diagonal stroke at *fig. 2,a.* This is why the corners must be avoided when drawing the first stroke, to accommodate the path.

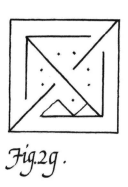

Fig.2g.

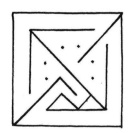

Fig.2,h.

Fig.2,i.

Fig.2,j.

On each arm of the arrowhead,
draw a zig-zag, fig.2,g, which locks
the "key", fig.2,h. Double the lock
and key, fig.2,i. Repeat diagonally opposite, fig.2,j.

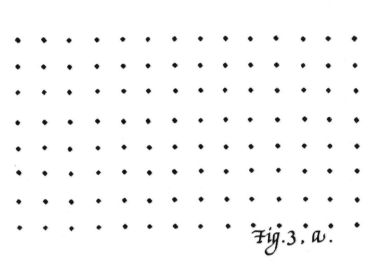

Fig.3, a.

N THE FOLLOWING PAGES, all the designs of *figs.* 3~6 are based on the grid above, which has Thirteen spaces across, and seven down.

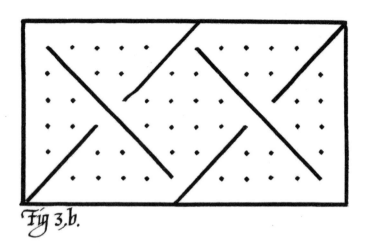

Fig 3,b.

On the grid lay the lines of the
diagonals as before, first the un-
broken stroke with a gap at each
end, as in *fig. 2a*, then the broken
diagonal, as in *fig. 2,b*. Complete the
right-hand half of *fig. 3,b* only after
having done the left side. Set off the
whole diagonal first, directly below
the intersection of the upper edge

[31]

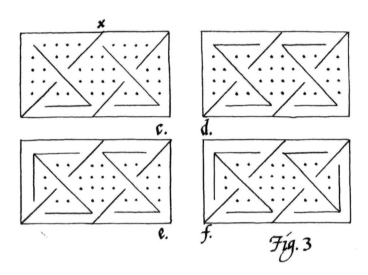

Fig. 3

with the broken diagonal already drawn, marked "x" above, f.3,c. Check that the positions of the diagonals are exactly as in f.3,b before proceeding. You can tell by the pattern of dots whether your lines are arranged correctly or not.

The next stage, the arrow-heads, includes two segments of path on

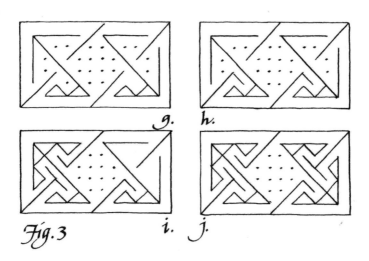

g. h.

Fig.3 i. j.

the upper and lower edge of the
rectangle, fig.3,f. This completes
the second stage. Check the dots
to ensure lines are in order.

Third, complete the corners, fig.3,
j. The keys are all aligned along the
edges. Only the centre diamond
cell remains. Notice the form of the
twelve dots in the diamond.

[33]

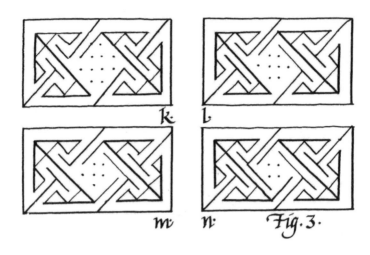

k. l.

m. n. Fig. 3.

There are quite a few variants that can be made in the central cell, but first, the swastika key pattern. In the diamond of fig. 3, j, you will see four paths leading into the space. Extend these paths, fig. 3, k–r, to form the clockwise spiral in the middle, in two stages. The first stage is shown here, k–n.

[34]

o. p.

Fig.3 q. r.

Make sure all four arms of the
spiral in fig. 3, n, are complete, and four
dots remain. Now wind a final turn,
as above, fig. 3, o-r.

The really significant part of this
pattern is the layout of the diagonals
and the keys around the edges and
corners. Master steps a-j, fig. 3, and
the following variations will be easy.

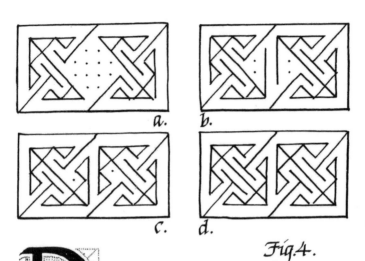

Fig.4.

DRAW the grid as in fig.3, and complete steps a~j up to the diamond with 12 dots, as above, fig.4,a.

Now complete the two arrow heads with a single path width between, as in fig.4,b.

Last, complete locks first, fig.4,c. either side of the vertical bar, fig.4,d.

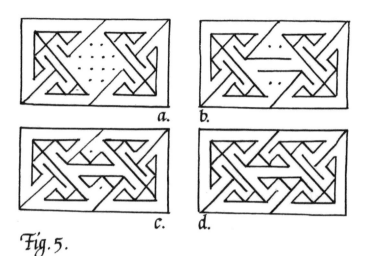

a. b.

c. d.

Fig. 5.

START This keypattern with the same build up as in the last one, but, instead of a vertical bar put in a horizontal, as in fig. 5,b, consisting of two parallel lines each springing from a key.

On the lines of the bar, put the zigzag lock, fig. 5c.

Complete key in each lock, fig. 5d.

[37]

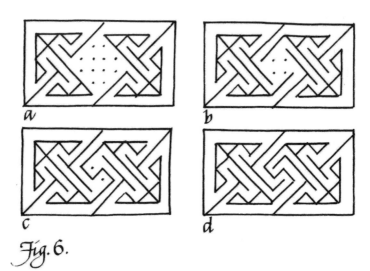

a

b

c

d

Fig. 6.

HERE the pattern follows fig. 3, a ~ n, to give the first turn of the clockwise spiral with four branches, fig. 6, b.

Two opposite branches may be connected by a zigzag stroke, fig. 6, c. These set off opposed locks.

Last, put keys in the locks, fig. 6, d.

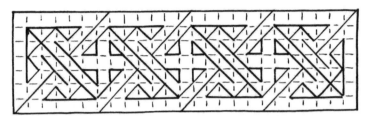

Fig. 7, a.

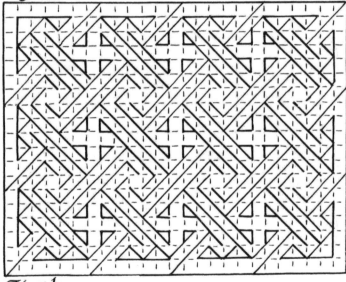

Fig. 7, b.

IGURES 1 to 6 in this intro-
ductory outline show how
the basic key pattern contains
in its structure the seeds of all
the mainstay variations used
by the ancient scribes. There are of
course other species sprung from
different seed structures, but
these more unusual key patterns
can wait for now.

Fig. 7, a, introduces another
diamond filler, in a repeat of four
basic units on a square grid seven
down and twenty-five across.

Fig. 7, b, is on a grid 25 x 19.

Leaving key patterns aside, for
now, let us take a look at spirals
with keys, let us play with spirals.

PIRALS: THE SINGLE SPIRAL.

Figure 1.

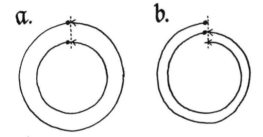

a.   b.

Compare the two figures above. The single spiral on the right turns twice, so it has the same effect as two concentric circles, fig.1, a; that is, the inside is surrounded by a path separating it from the outside.

[41]

Single Spiral : s~scroll.

Fig.2

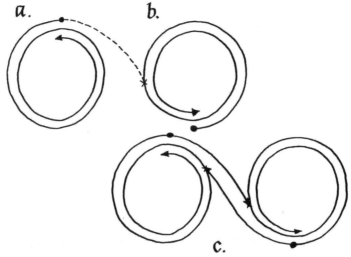

a.   b.

c.

Two singles joined so the path leads from one to the other. Notice how the spiral at f.2,a, starts at the top, and f.2,b, starts at the bottom.

The path connecting the spirals is drawn with two lines. The first joins the outside of the path of the first spiral, f.2,a, to the inside of the second, f.2,b, as shown dotted here. The second line joins the bottom of b to the inside of the first spiral, f.2,c. The path now leads from the inside of one spiral to the empty centre of the second. This integrates the design so that it may not be entered from without, being completely self-contained. In traversing the spiralling path you begin at the centre and end at the centre. We cannot expand further on this design externally, but we may elaborate the middle spaces.

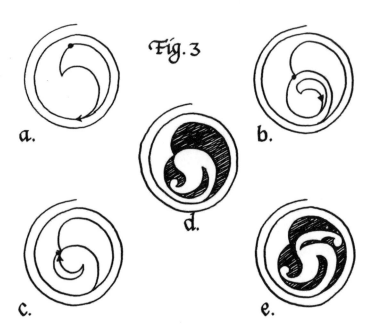

Fig. 3

a.

b.

c.

d.

e.

ere you have five variations, all developed from the "comma" path ending, f. 3a, from which are derived f.s 3, b,c.

Figures 3,d and e are types of "duck-head" terminal. Figure 3,e is a "triskel".

Fig. 4

The spirals on this s-scroll are identical, based on *fig. 3,b*. One is upside down in relation to the other. Any spiral in *fig. 3* may be treated as an s-scroll. A counter may be drawn to relieve the largest background space - such as the "eye" used here. This should not be overdone: one counter per largest background space is sufficient in most instances.

In *fig. 4* there is a second type of counter, to be used only where the path flares widest, called a "lens".

Fig. 5

The spiral on the left is the same as at fig. 3, d, the "duck-head" terminal. Three lenses have been added in each duck-head, plus one at the widest point of the path. Inside the widest part of each spiral's background is a counter circle, containing two lenses. Between the two spirals the path diverges, at which point a bracketed lens, or "trumpet mouth", is used to counter the path's width.

The s-scroll may be enclosed with lines. The background is also countered.

[46]

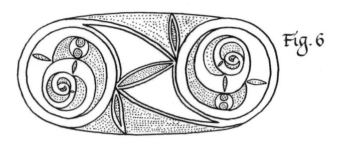

Fig. 6

In this figure, the path between the spirals has been made as wide as can be. With the path so wide as this, the centre lens may be outlined as shown, and the outline continued back along the path.

With so much path, the lenses either side of the cross over have been in-lined and filled-in, to counter as much as possible of the outer background.

Inside the spiral roundels the counter used - that looks like an apple-core-is called

SINGLE SPIRAL DUCK-HEAD
TERMINAL *from*
TORRS PONY CAP

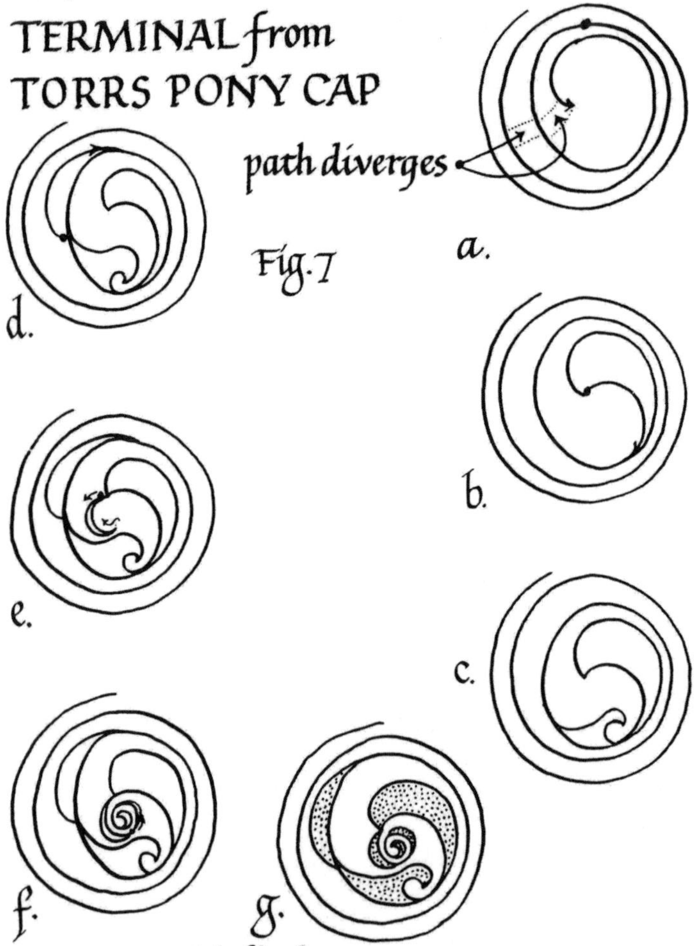

path diverges

Fig. 7

a.

b.

c.

d.

e.

f.

g.

Compare with fig. 8, opp.

a "labrys", but as the labrys has many other forms, I shall call this one "the apple-core".

One of the earliest forms of the duck-head appears in the N. British school of Celtic metal work that produced the Torrs Pony Cap, about 250 B.C. The basic design may be drawn in one continuous stroke as shown in fig. 7, a–d.

Fig. 8

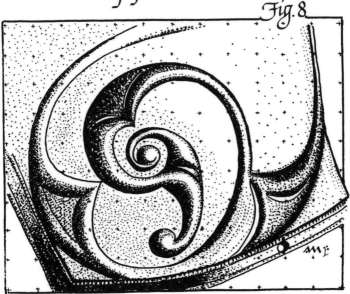

Fig. 8 shows a detail from the Torrs Pony Cap. The design is the prototype of spiral roundels that reach their fullest flowering 1000 years later in the Book of Kells. Modern Celtic artists wishing to develop the tradition further should first grasp the essentials of the art by a close study of the earliest forms such as underlie the later developments.

Fig. 9

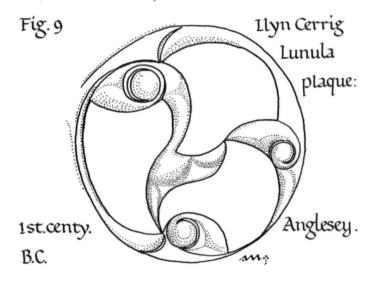

Llyn Cerrig Lunula plaque:

1st. centy. B.C.

Anglesey.

Fig. 10

Fig. 10, for example, seems to be a complete departure from the tradition, but in fact, it is based on the Llyn Cerrig roundel, Fig. 9. The pattern here is based on petal shapes, freely drawn and randomly grouped. The petal comes from the shape between the spirals in the basic s~scroll, Fig. 11.

Fig. 11
From circular box lid,
La Tène period, 1st. cent. B.C.,
Cornalaragh, Co. Monaghan.

[51]

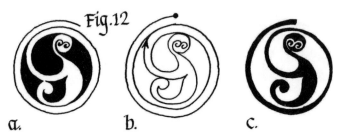

F.12, duck-head type terminal, Torrs
Pony Cap. Background and fore-
ground are interchangable, f.12,a,c.
Single stroke construction also
shown at f.12,b.

Fig.13.
a.

b.

Fig.14

The single line construction appears in this design from Balmaclellan, Kircudbrightshire, c. 30 A.D., f. 13, 14. This is also a series of double spirals, ending in a single spiral, extreme right, f. 13. See also the border below, which starts and ends in single spirals, f. 15.

Fig.15

Double spirals in an s-scroll oval, or "cartouche".

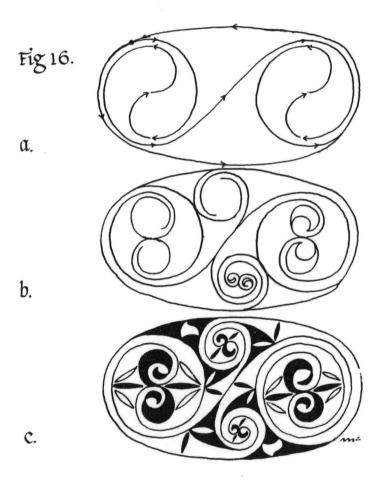

Fig 16.

a.

b.

c.

Fig. 17

Fig. 18

Fig. 19

Compare f.17 with f.10; and compare f.s. 18, 19 with f.13.

a. single, 3 turns

b. double 1½ trns

c.

d.

e.

f.

g.

h.

i.

j.

k.

Fig. 20 Double spirals, "c-scroll".

1,3, Battersea; 2, Neath.
4,7, unprovenanced.
5, Witham; 6, Thames.

8, King's Langley.
9,10, Brentford.
11,12, Mayer; 13, Birdlip.
14, Polden Hill.
15, Brentwood; 16, Woodeaton.

1. Thames   2. polden hill   3. Dolphintail [2]

4. Neath, Birdlip   5. Nijmegan   6. Nijmegan

7. Desborough, Birdlip   8. Trelan Bahaw   9. woodeaton

early Celtic Spirals

1. Suffolk terret

2. Battersea

3. Polden hill

4. Battersea

5. St-Mawgan-in-Pyder

6. Polden Hill

7. Mayer

8. Cornalaragh

9. Broighter torque

10. Lakenheath

11. Mayer

12. Shannon Cup

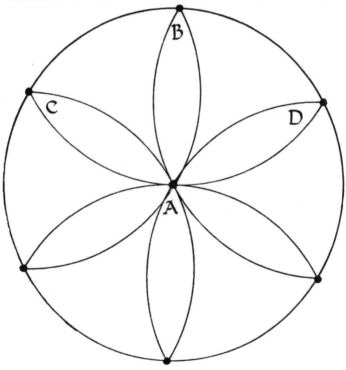

D raw circle, centre A, page 60.
With same radius, and centre
B, draw arc, C D. Keeping same radius
step off the six points, and join in
the form of a star as here:

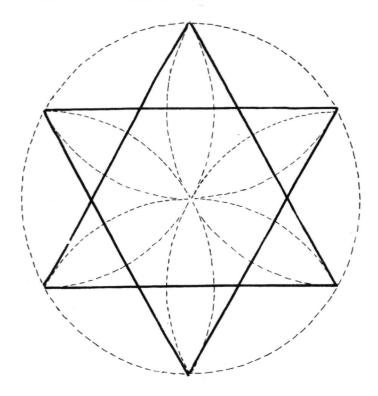

H ere the star is used to construct a triangular grid. This grid is used to construct four circles, opposite.

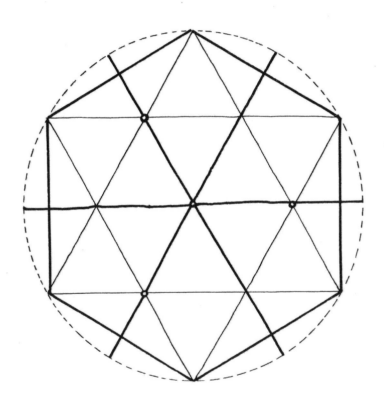

The distance between the intersection of the star triangles &
the outer hexagon, AB, provides us
with the radius for close-packed
circles.

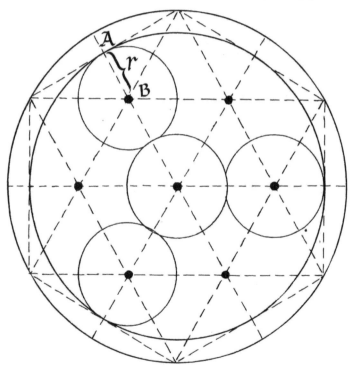

S imilarly, seven circles may be packed together.

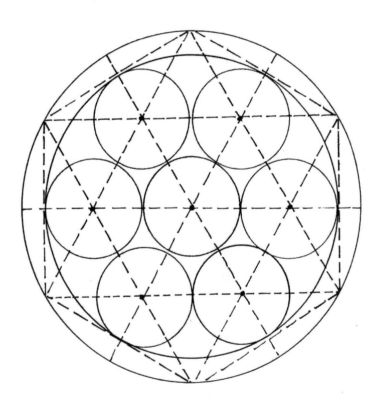

Each circle contains a star. So the whole is reflected in the parts. Triple spirals may be placed in the shaded stars, as will be shown.

Chapter IV

With centres A,B,C draw arcs DE,FG,HI. These arcs will connect the triple spirals.

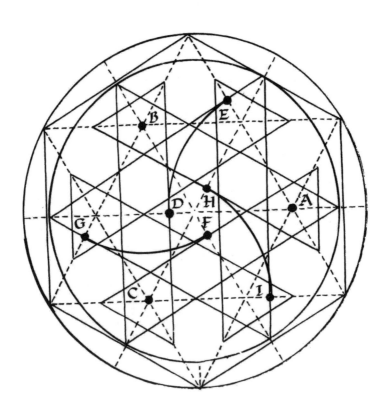

O ther arcs, all with radius JK,
may be set off from centres
J, M, N and O.

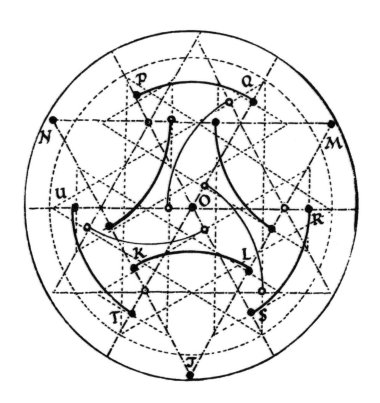

Here the ends of the arcs have been wound into spirals, double and triple. The result is a regular design of continuous line spirals.

By the addition of three sets of three arcs, the line spirals are converted into interlocking c-scroll paths. The arcs supply bulges in the passages from spiral to spiral.

The roundel on the previous page has three double spirals. The addition of one more coil to each of these makes an overall triple spiral, composed of triples, linked together in opposed pairs.

Geometry of the spiral

As seen above, page 65, the whole is reflected in the parts in the geometry of circle, hexagon & star, the same geometry as generates the triple spiral roundel, opposite and here beneath:

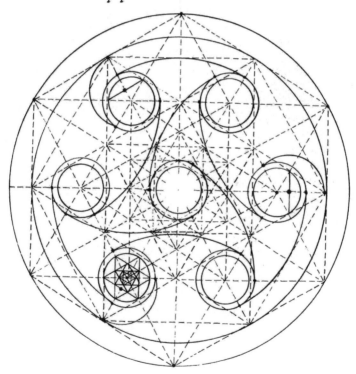

Chapter IV

WITH this in view it follows that the whole triple spiral design may be reflected in each of the triples contained within it, thus:

irish

abcd
efs
hijk
lmn
opq
rstu
vwxyz

half

uncial

script

Alphabet written with Speedball nib, C-1.

[73]

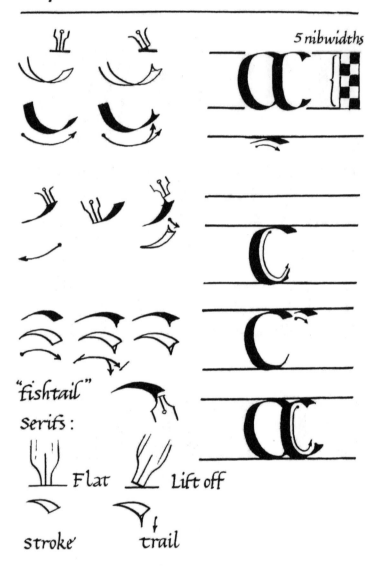

5 nibwidths

"fishtail"
serifs:

Flat   Lift off

stroke   trail

---

ascender, 2½ nib widths.
"x" height, five n.w's.

Flag serifs, on tops of
straight, vertical strokes only,
except for 'b' and 'l', which
begin straight, then
curve.
Letters b, upright d,
f, h, i, j, k, l, m, n, p, q, r,
u, (v), w, (y), all have
flag serifs. While
Fishtails are optional,
flag serifs are not.

For the most part, except for serif and foot pen–
twists, pen angle should approach a 20° constant.

1.

c.

d: two forms, both equally
traditional

2.

twist pen from 20°
to level foot.

optional construction

Use one d or another, not both in same text.

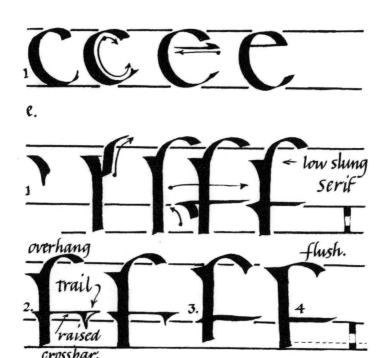

e.

← low slung serif

overhang

flush.

trail

raised crossbar.

f: several versions, 4 is the most compact.

eg, et – this type of tall letter e is used before t and g.

[77]

1. Crossbar corresponds to that of t.

G: version 2 is a suggested modernisation.

h.

The tail serif on the celtic g may be trailed with the left hand corner of the nib. The modernised form is based on q, below, and may be used with q, 1.

[78]

i: the final downstroke may be given a final twist to level the foot from 20°–horizontal.

j, 3 variations:

1.

2: a modernised version.

2.

3.

3: this foot is borrowed from that of the letter q, see below.

Triangular foot may be drawn by twisting pen, or added on with a small pointed nib, such as a crow-quill.

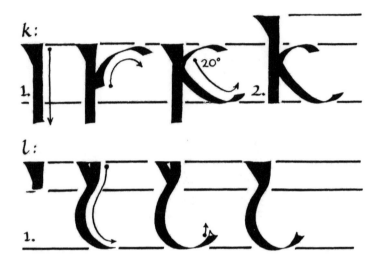

There is no letter k in the original Celtic mss., so one of the challenges is to supply missing letters, j, k, v, w, as well as to modernise the archaic ones, particularly g, q, t, and y. Here the first k is very compatible with the old forms, while k 2 is slightly modern looking.

[80]

m:

1.

2.

m; two variants, the first is the regular one, the second only for use as the first letter of a word. The point to remember about the letter m is that its arches are much narrow than the arch of n or h.

[81]

1. This form relates to the letter, h.

2.

This form is very much a majuscule;

the slant may sometimes come above the
right foot; the left foot may descend a little.

These two n's, however, should not be used in
the same text. Use one or the other.

o:

p.

1

2.

twist pen.

3

q, 3 variations: the first two are traditional. the third is a modern version, with a reversal of the foot; this last may be used with g, 2, above, as may q,1.

1. 2.

3. This r may be
used in conjunction
with n, 2.

1.

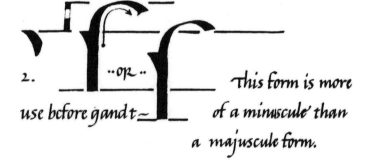

2. ..or..

use before g and t~ This form is more
of a minuscule than
a majuscule form.

t.

1.

2.

The difference between u, 1 and 2 is that the first is pulled straight from the serif into the curve; the second bends to the left, rather than being pulled down straight.

v: two variations: these are suggestions only.

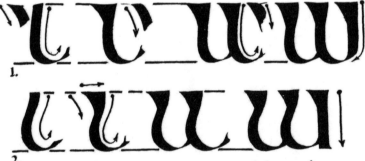

w: variation 2 is the more traditional in
style.

x , 5 variations:

1.

20°

2.

3.

4.

5.

3 variations, y ,:

1.

2.

3.

z : like many of the letters in this alphabet, z allows for a number of mutations, whereby the pen may be given free play. Here, 3, 4, 6 are variants of 1, while 5 is a variant of 2.

HOW TO LAY OUT A MANUSCRIPT PAGE ✦

ONCE YOU

are familiar with the letters of any
particular script it is best to select a
text and produce a single~page manuscript, or a number of such pages.
A text may be written over many
times, and may be improved a little each time; you can develop a sense
of design by doing this, and produce
work that truly pleases you, that
you may include in your portfolio,
or present, suitably matted and
mounted of course, to a friend.

IRST you need a lot of paper. It need not be very special but it is worth getting a batch of good, non-acid, not too thin, smooth, white paper. 2-ply "Bristol board" does quite well. Stock up with 50 or 100 sheets from an art supplies outlet. A good size is 36" x 28". Store paper flat, wrapped up safe from damp, dust, pawmarks, and such. A closet may be adapted to paper storage by putting in shelves.

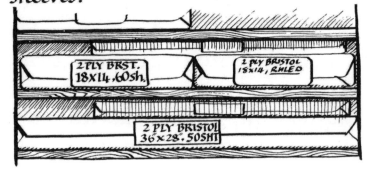

WHEN you buy a stock of
paper in a whole or broken
packet, keep it in its wrap-
per until ready to use. Remove as
many sheets as you need, close up the
remainder and return to storage.
Keep the sheets in the same order as
they came from the package, same
face up, same corner alignment.
Pencil lightly a mark in the upper
left hand corner, to help keep the
sheets in order. One side of the paper, for instance, is sometimes better than the other to write on, and
you will want to find out which before ruling up your single pages,
so as to stack the pages with the
better side up.

MEASURING THE PAPER FOR CUTTING

TAKE ONE SHEET & MEASURE IT 18" along one side, 14" the other. If your sheet is 36" x 28" to begin with, it will quarter economically to a standard 18" x 14" page; if not, trim it down.

MARKING THE CUTTING MAT.

TRIMMING A LOT OF PAGES
 may be done more easily
on a cutting mat, a sheet of
dense card or illustration board
at least ⅛" thick, 4' x 3'. On this,
pencil the 36" x 28" area, divide
each side and quarter the area.
Having checked the lines and angles, ink in the marks for the
corners and the cuts to be made.

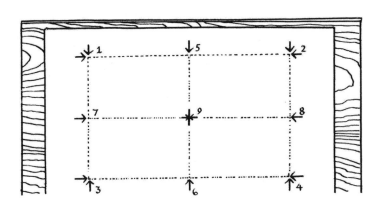

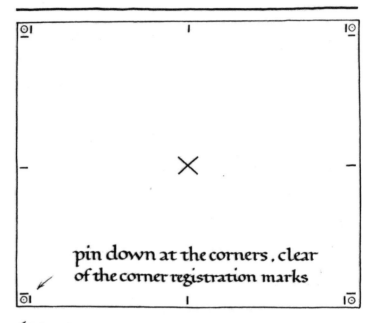

pin down at the corners, clear
of the corner registration marks

TAKE THE CUTTING MAT,
marked up as illustrated above;
lay it on a board, and pin it down.
For the board, a sheet of plywood,
4' x 3', will do – get the lumber
yard to cut down an 8' x 4' sheet to
a couple of boards; both will prove
handy to have about the studio.

[94]

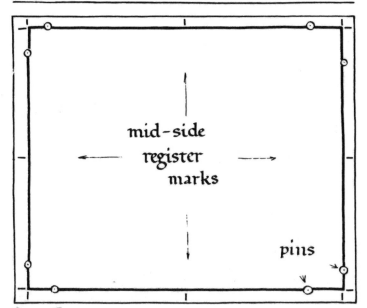

mid-side
register
marks

pins

N OW TAKE A NUMBER OF
sheets; squared up, stacked
and lined up on the cutting mat
with the corner registration marks.
Pin down the stack with old-fash-
ioned, large-headed drawing pins;
pin clear of the register marking
the mid-point of each side.

When you pin the stack of pages, do not pierce the paper with the shaft of the pin. The head of the pin only should hold the paper. The bigger the pin-head, the better.

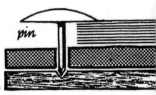

pin

The sort of blade you snap off is very handy.

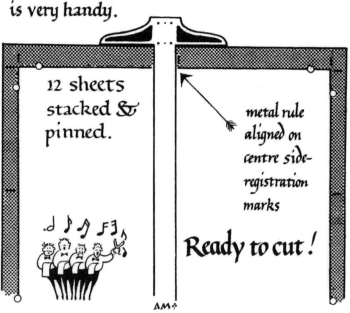

12 sheets stacked & pinned.

metal rule aligned on centre side-registration marks

Ready to cut!

AM

paper
cutting mat
base board

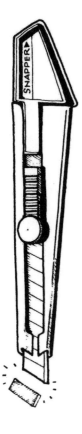

Never use a wood or plastic edged ruler when cutting; a metal edged or all-metal ruler is a must for all cutting jobs.

When cutting, press down on the ruler with one hand, but do not press on the knife any more than is needed to cut through a single sheet at a time, for the most accurate result. Remove the cut sheets one by one.

Make the first cut from top to bottom. Then cut from side to side, according to the registration marks. Snap off the blade, half-way through.

[97]

NOW YOU HAVE CUT A dozen sheets, 36"x 28", into four dozen pages, 14"x 18", or an ample supply of standard-size stock of paper suitable for single-page manuscript, enough to last a year.

You also have your studio equipped to handle most cutting jobs. The board and mat set-up will be re-used as is. Store it flat against the wall until it is needed again.

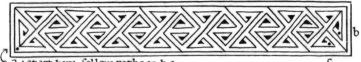

a : start here, follow paths to b,c.

NEXT the page must be ruled for writing, but ruling can become tiresome and off-putting, whereas a number of pages may be ruled all at the same time by means of a simple template.

HOW TO MAKE A TEMPLATE FOR RULING

RULE one sheet first, in pencil, according to the plan illustrated on the next page. This is the master layout for the template, and therefore should be made as carefully as can be. Check the corners and the intersections with the T-square and set square to be sure the right angles are true.

THE RULES' spacing given here is standardised to the proportions of a nib width of $\frac{1}{16}$".

We will use a Celtic script, of which the letter 'o' is five nib widths high. The rules are three 'o's' apart, or $\frac{15}{16}$".

2½" 2½"

2½"

1 this is what a line of script
2 will look like.
3 rules are three 'o's apart.
3 'o's { 8 4

$\frac{15}{16}$"

5 ---- ⊢ 0 = $\frac{5}{16}$"
6
7
8
9
10
11
12
13
14

The page is 14"x18"

The

script. ;

abcdef

ghijkl

mnopq

Rstuv

wxyz⁊

WHEN you have this page all ruled up, you can use it to rule up a number of other pages, as a template. To make the template, with a pin, prick holes through the page where the rules for the lines cross the margins. With a pencil you can trans fer the points on to a second sheet placed directly beneath the template. Removing the template, the second sheet may be ruled up according to the transferred guide points. Like - wise, the template may be re-used to rule any number of single-page manuscript pages.

Or, with a fine, strong pin, you may prick through several sheets at once.

HOW TO
DECORATE
LETTERS

I, n, o, ë, and l

FIRST OF ALL WE NEED some letters to decorate. They may be drawn, as on the following pages. Here I have simplified the old Irish letters, called Majuscules, and presented them in a proportion which is based on a 5^2 grid.

A ll the letter forms on these pages are intended as models for drawing the outlines of outsize letters to be illuminated with Celtic ornament.

I have given the grid as based on a square divided into five on each side, or 5x5, because I have found this to have had special significance to early illuminators, such as those of the Lindisfarne Gospels. Also, this gives a good proportion between the width of the stroke and height, as of the letter 'i', for instance: $1/5$. With the addition of the outline, this proportion approximates the Lindisfarne ideal nibwidth: i-height, $1:4\frac{1}{2}$.

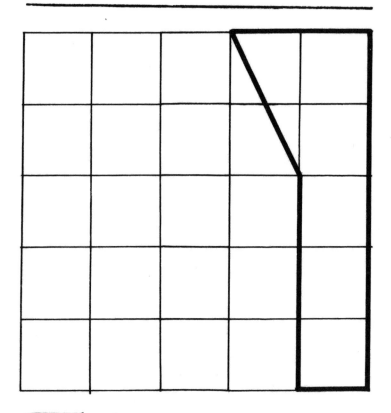

The side of the square is the height of the letter 'I', as here, or width of an 'O', page 111, below. If it were pen-written, it would be 5 nib widths high.

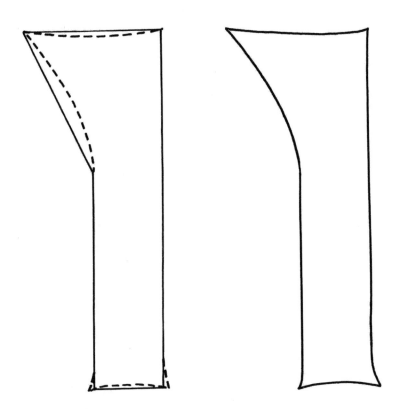

The grid gives us a standard proportion for majuscules, as well as the ideal flag serif. The angles may curve a little, as here.

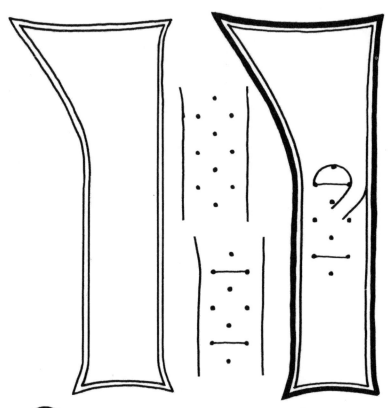

Outline the letter; thicken up the outline; add another outline. Colour the interior lightly and brightly – or put in a knot.

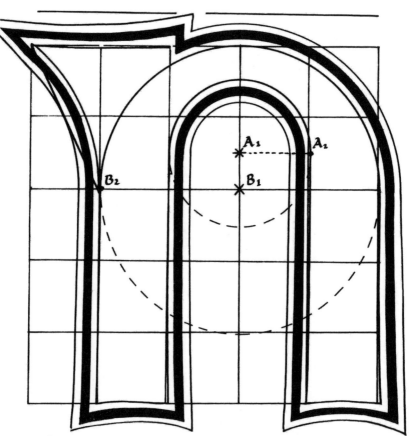

After I, the letter N may be an-
alysed on a 5² grid. This figure
may be followed as a model in
free-hand drawing, or as a geometric

exercise. With compasses and ruler
the entire letter may be produced.
The centre band may be coloured.

O, too, may be built with compasses, next page. Note the
knot construction. The
inner void is filled with steps.

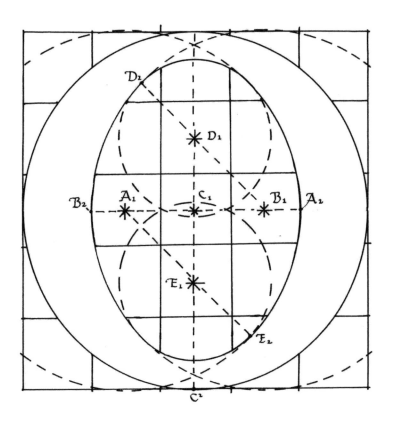

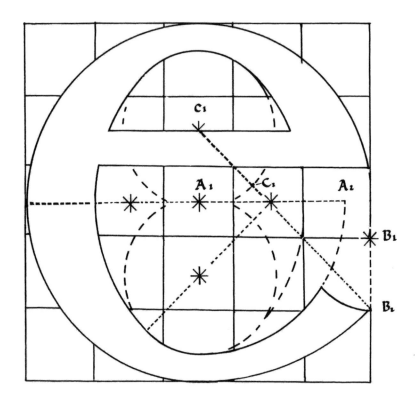

E follows the geometry of O, but for the curve of the tail; A_1A_2; C_1B_2. If not following the geometry, use squared paper to plot the

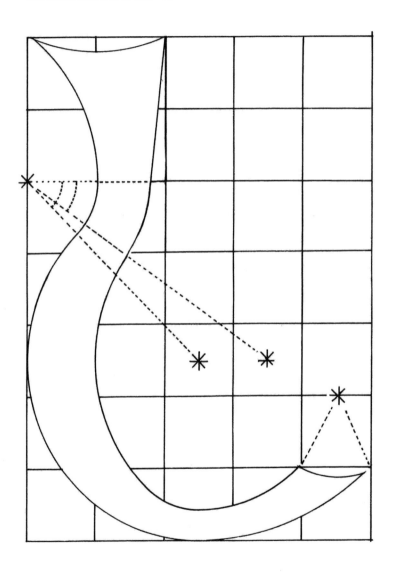

letters, trace and transfer.

The form of the majuscule L, overleaf follows from E, and introduces our grid for ascenders, b d h l , and descenders, ꝼ ᵹ ı ꝁ p ꝗ x y ᵹ : 5 x 7. The descender of ꝼ, ꝁ, x, ᵹ is characteristic of the archaic script. Now f, k, are ascenders, while x, z have joined the mid-height tribe based on i : m, n, ꞃ, u, w; and on o : c, e, s, ꞇ, x.

IT may also be remarked that here the letters are not capitals, to which we are accustomed; but although the old ꝏ, b, c, ꝺ, e, ꝼ ᵹ, h, ı, ꝁ look like small letters, or minuscules they originally had the status and dignity of formal capitals.

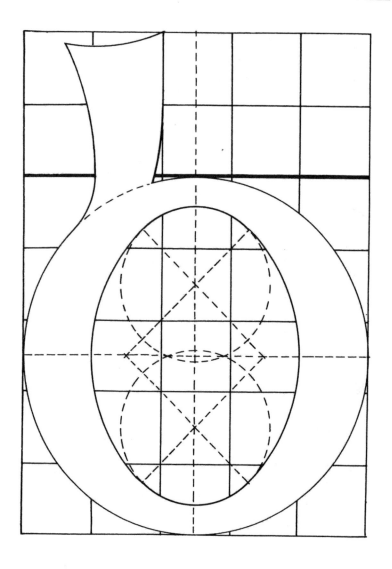

[115]

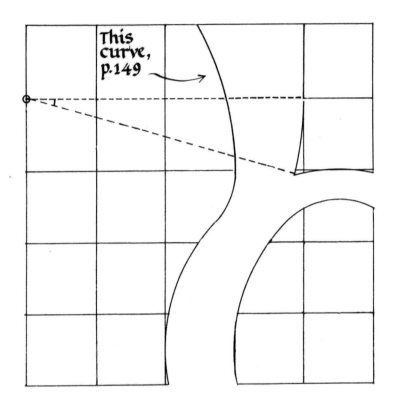

This
curve,
p.149

COMPARE the top of the
B with that of L, p. 113.
This narrower, blunter
serif is preferable.

WHILE the body of B follows from O, the D stems from C. C has the same tail as E. H is likewise close to N, p. 108 & 120.

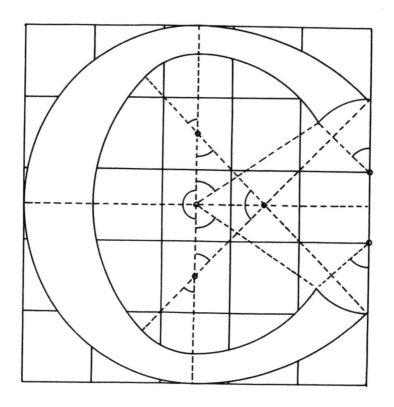

[117]

T here are two curves to the serif of D.
This concludes the ascenders.
Next, 121–129, the descenders: F, G, J, K, P, Q, X, Y, Z.

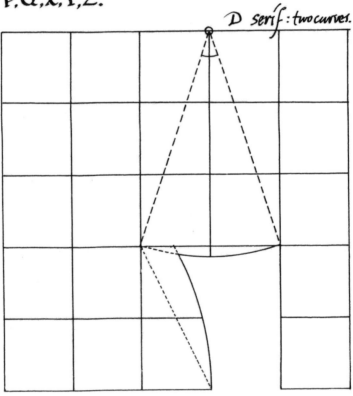

D serif: two curves.

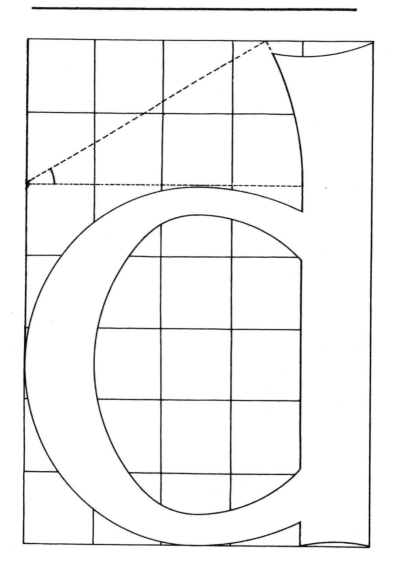

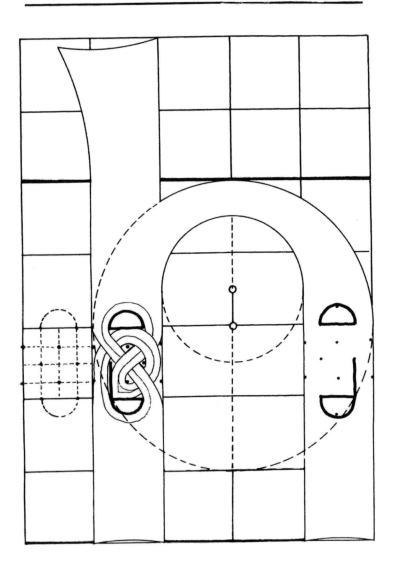

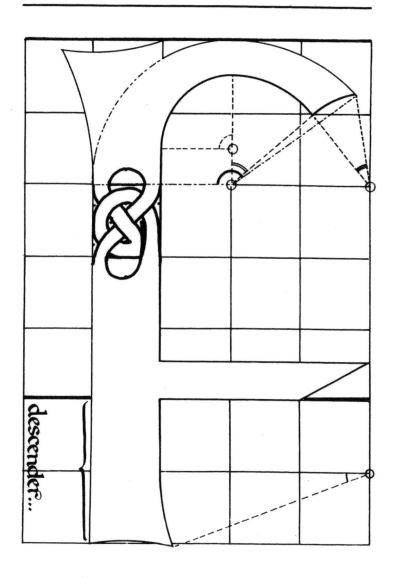

descender...

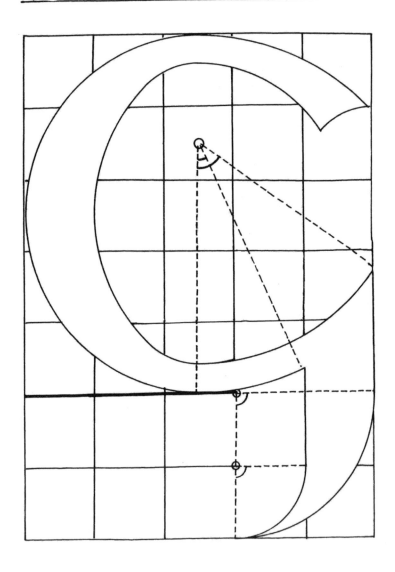

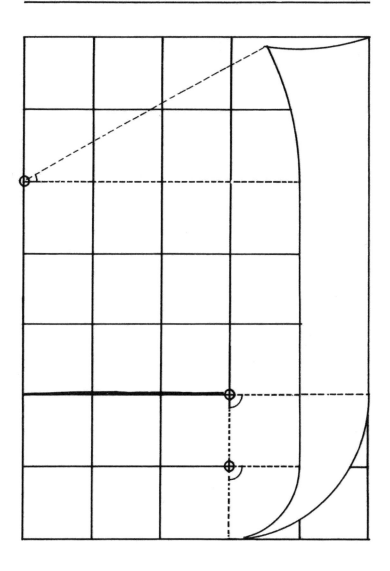

[123]

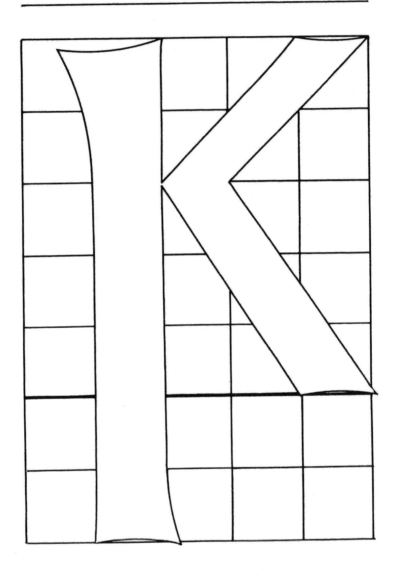

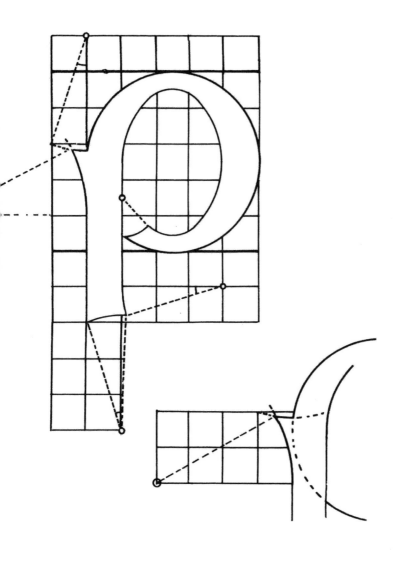

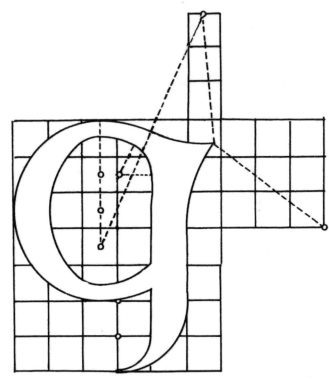

Y ES, this is Q, in the Celtic alphabet. It can be given a flat foot to match P, too.

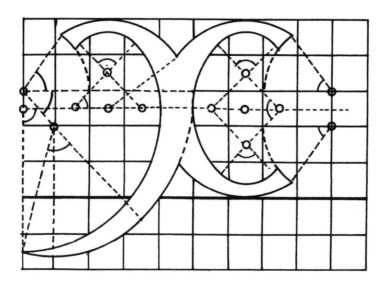

The X is a descender, as we
see here. Each half is a cut-
off O, with the tail added,
sweeping away below leftwards. Or,
equally, it could be done symmet-
rically; the left reflecting the right.

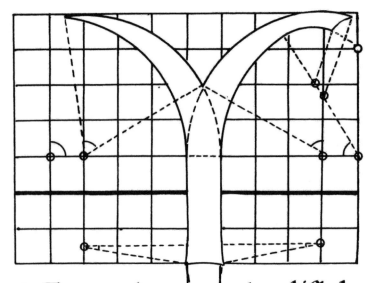

HERE is a simplified form of Y, with a straight descen- der. This foot is quite symmetrical. A curve, as in Q, would do as well. The sharp prong could be re—

peated on the right .. Y, like G, is
pretty versa-
tile. So is the
celtic ZED:
those dots
are centres
for drawing
the success -
ion of arcs

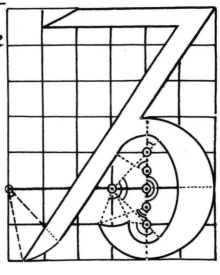

that may be compass drawn to produce the spiral tail.

WHICH brings up the point,
WHY bother with the geometry
at all?

[129]

As forms, letters are pen-made shapes. When a letter is to be decorated, however, it may be drawn freely or with compasses. Many including myself find it easier to draw a straight line with a ruler, a curve with compasses. So here is an alphabet of letters produced by compasses and ruler entirely. By this means, sharp, controlled, well-proportioned and lively shapes may be obtained. Few can do this freehand on a large scale, so here the letters are given along with their geometry. Besides, it really is fun to do, and compass work is an essential element of early Celtic art. This is good practice.

As well as ascenders and descenders there are the letters with neither, namely:

aceim

orstu

vwnd*

* this letter has two forms, an ascender, d, and the flattened
form, ɒ, as here.

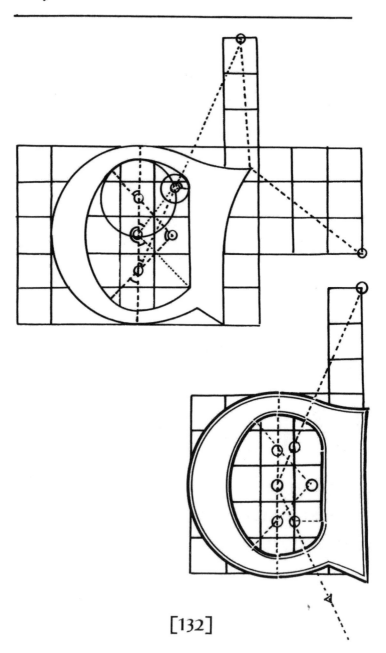

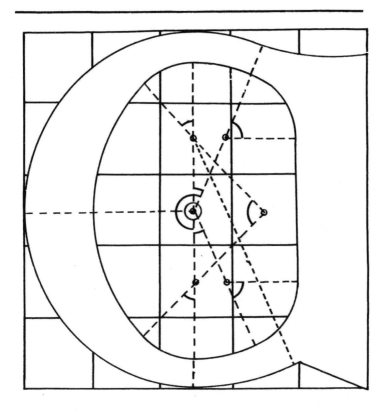

This page, as below, opposite, a simple form of the Celtic letter, ɑ. Opposite, above, a variation of the serif, like that of ꝺ, on page 126. 𝕫

INSTEAD of decorating the letter
with a plain knot, it can be
done with animal-shaped, zoomorph-
ic pattern based on a knot, as here.
Each snake has two long ears, laced
into the weaving body-ribbons.

1.   2.   3.   4.

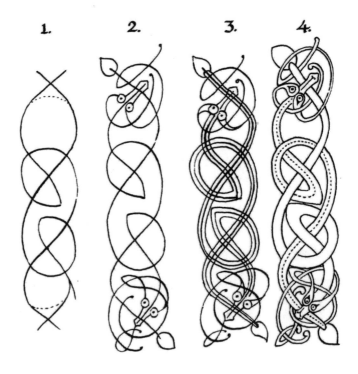

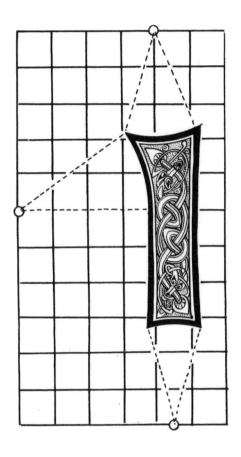

construction
of the knot
used here in
the snakes.

[135]

R: • The stem of this letter is • made the same way as 'l'. The curve uses five centres, 3 for the outside, top left, opposite page. HERE'S HOW: draw the arc 1, with the compasses fixed at centre 1. With the same centre, repeat the curve of the outline; step the fixed point to centre 2 and draw arc 2, inline and outline; continue arc 3 with centre 3.

FOR the inside curve, keep the centre at 3, and draw inside curve 3, see figure lower right. Continue the inline (thin) and outline (thick) through curve and centre 4 : ditto from centre 5.

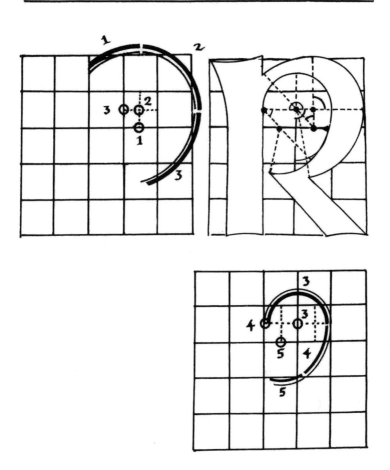

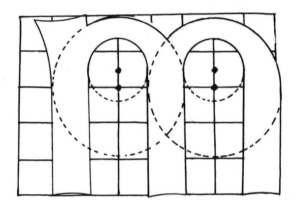

m: the steps for drawing
'm' are as follows:
lightly pencil a grid, 8 x 5.
Draw the stem, as for 'l'.
Pencil the circles, straight rule
the legs.
Extend the grid to draw the
hollows on the head & feet serifs,

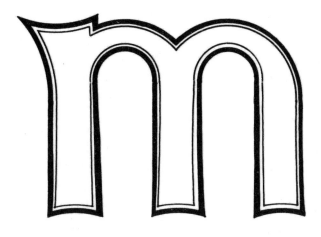

as shown on page 135.
In drawing the letter, start at a
point, say upper left, then draw
each curved line or straight line
section continuously, each new
line starting precisely on and
springing from the end of the
last one; progress around the out-

[139]

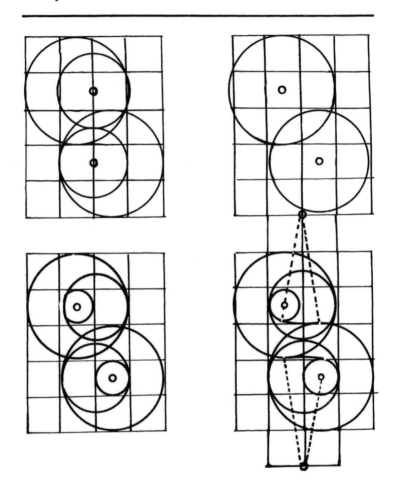

line, doing thin and thick lines
together. Then repeat, in ink.

S: • first pencil
• the circles as
on page 140,
then the head and
tail, here, above.
The waist can be
done from two centres,
making it concave,
or from one centre
as here, below.
All the centres may
be found from points
on the grid, or the
crossing of lines
between established
centres.

[141]

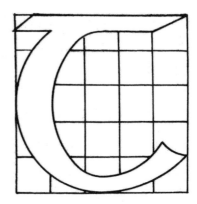

T: the body of 'T' is like 'C' on page 117 above.

U: opposite: extend the square grid to make the head and foot serifs on letters such as 'U'. If you are inking up the letter close to the edge of the page and find you have not enough room, you can extend the page by slipping another sheet alongside and partly under the first, and taping it.

[142]

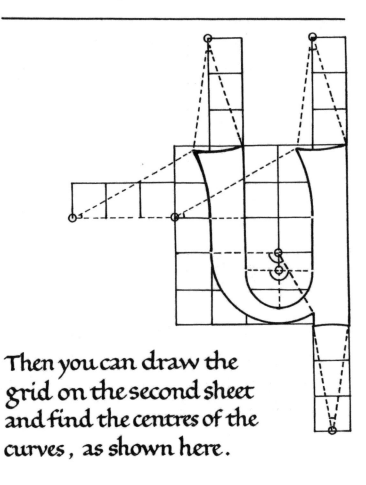

Then you can draw the
grid on the second sheet
and find the centres of the
curves, as shown here.

W :

here the letter is made up
of 'U', as on the previous page.
Another form is the 'Double-Vee',
as opposite, above.

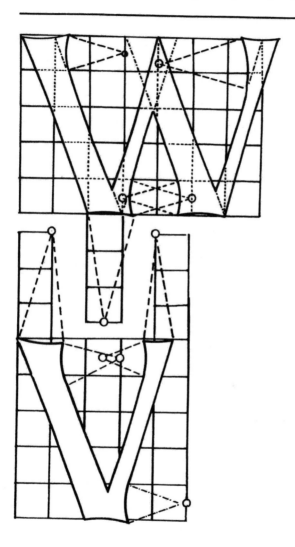

[145]

Conclusion

The letters here may be decorated with step patterns or key patterns. Use the illuminated letters you make as initials, personalised monograms, greeting cards, gift labels, fabric paintings etc. The patterns may be used in themselves wherever ornamentation is called for in art or in decor; in textiles, tiles, metalwork, woodwork, murals; the applications are as many as may be imagined. With pen and paper you can easily master the patterns in this book. Then look around and apply them in your own life, however you may feel inspired. The aim of this book, and that of the entire series of "Celtic Design", will thereby be fulfilled: the revival of Celtic art. ✝

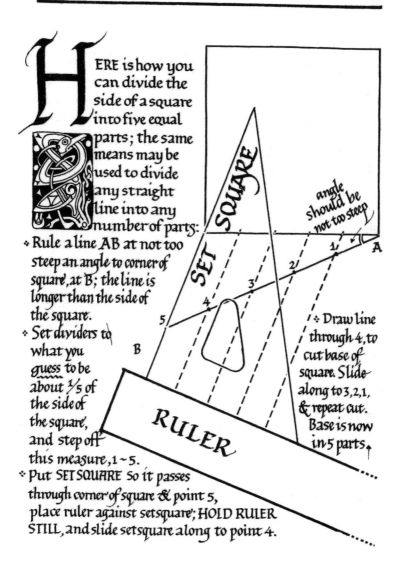

HERE is how you can divide the side of a square into five equal parts; the same means may be used to divide any straight line into any number of parts:

* Rule a line AB at not too steep an angle to corner of square, at B; the line is longer than the side of the square.

* Set dividers to what you guess to be about ⅕ of the side of the square, and step off this measure, 1~5.

* Put SET SQUARE so it passes through corner of square & point 5, place ruler against setsquare; HOLD RULER STILL, and slide setsquare along to point 4.

* Draw line through 4, to cut base of square. Slide along to 3, 2, 1, & repeat cut. Base is now in 5 parts↑

angle should be not too steep

SET SQUARE

RULER

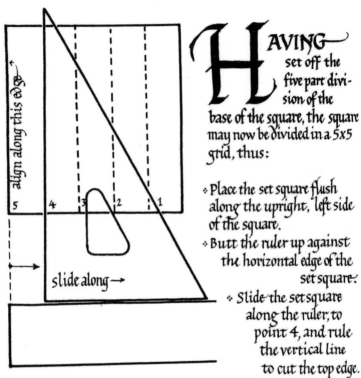

align along this edge →

5   4   3   2   1

slide along →

HAVING set off the five part division of the base of the square, the square may now be divided in a 5x5 grid, thus:

∴ Place the set square flush along the upright, left side of the square.
∴ Butt the ruler up against the horizontal edge of the set square.
∴ Slide the set square along the ruler, to point 4, and rule the vertical line to cut the top edge.

∴ Now slide along the ruler to point 3, and rule across the square to cut the upper edge.
∴ Carry on until the square is divided by lines cutting through points 2 and 1.
∴ N.B. throughout, keep ruler steady. If it moves, move the set square back to the edge and butt the ruler back into line.

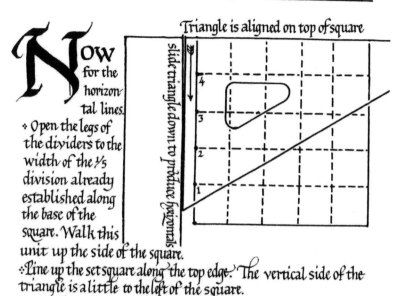

Triangle is aligned on top of square

slide triangle down to produce horizontals

Now for the horizontal lines.

❖ Open the legs of the dividers to the width of the ⅕ division already established along the base of the square. Walk this unit up the side of the square.

❖ Line up the set square along the top edge. The vertical side of the triangle is a little to the left of the square.

❖ Butt the ruler against the upright side of the square.

❖ Using the ruler as a guide track, slide the triangle down to point 4, and draw the horizontal across.

❖ Likewise, produce remaining latitudinal parallel lines at points 3,2,1, to complete the 5×5 grid.

The grid can be extended beyond the square with the ruler, by projecting the horizontal and vertical lines. To make a grid 8 across and 5 down, first extend the square by producing all the horizontal lines. Step off the ⅕ of the square to three spaces as before; place ruler horizontally below the figure as on previous page, as a rail along which to slide the setsquare and thus complete the grid.

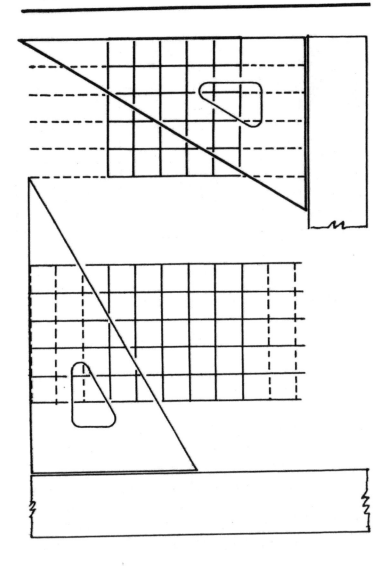

 HE set square and ru-
ler may be used to
extend a grid on either
side of the square, not only to
lay out a wide letter, but also to
find centres for serifs and such
which may lie off the area to
one side or the other. With a pair
of dividers, a set square and a straight edge, a grid may be extended
indefinitely, horizontally or verti-
cally. As Celtic patterns are based
normally on grids, it is necessary
to know how to construct such a
grid. The alphabet here presented
provides an opportunity to develop skill with these tools of design.

[151]

Appendix

SE the triangle to layout
a page of text like this :
with the top of the page
as a horizontal, and the
triangle flush with this, set the corner
of the set square to the left of the left-
hand margin and set the ruler
against the vertical side of the triangle. Hold the ruler firmly between
thumb and middle finger, slide the
triangle down to the point on the
margin line for the top of the text, and
hold it there with the index finger of
the left hand; the finger on the triangle
need not press as heavily as the two on
the ruler. With the right hand, draw
the horizontal rule, while the left

holds the ruler & triangle steady.
Should the ruler's slip, begin again. It
may slip if you relax your pressure
on the ruler, forgetfully. This initial
tendency is remedied by practice. If
the ruler swivels, however, it may
be bowed, and should therefore be
discarded and replaced. If you use
wood rulers, get two at a time, to
cover the possibility of warpage in
one of them.

Having ruled the horizontal line
marking the head of the text, next do
the vertical margin lines: move the
triangle to the corner of the text area,
upper left, flush with the horizontal.

Appendix

A : to establish the upper edge of the text block, place triangle along top of page; butt the ruler against the vertical edge of the triangle; hold the ruler in place with thumb and middle finger. }

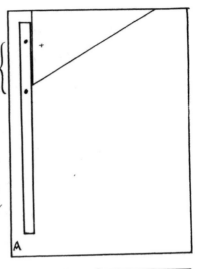

B : slide the triangle along the ruler to where you have decided the top of the text should be. Do this with one hand, keeping a firm pressure on the ruler all the while with thumb and finger. When the triangle is in position, hold it with the index finger of the hand holding the ruler. Thus one hand holds both ruler and set square, which leaves the other free to pencil the horizontal line atop the text block.

C : the horizontal line now becomes the guide for the left hand margin: slide the triangle over so that its corner coincides with that of the text block; butt the ruler against the set square; hold the ruler, take away the triangle, and rule the vertical.

D : likewise, the other side.

E : step the line spacing off on the left with the dividers.

F : mark the lower case "x-height" above the top line; with the dividers still at the line spacing as before, step off the spacing; with ruler and setsquare, rule.

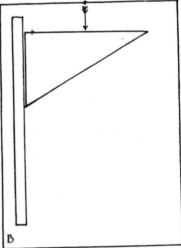

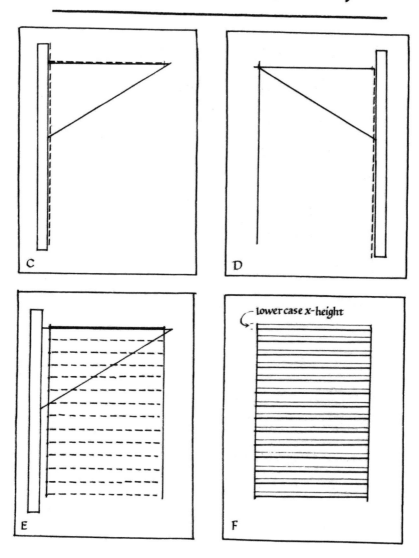

C

D

E

F

lower case x-height

Appendix

Dividers: this tool is used to divide a line into a number of equal spaces, as in ruling a page. In this case, the spacing is de‐termined by the width of the pen's nib.

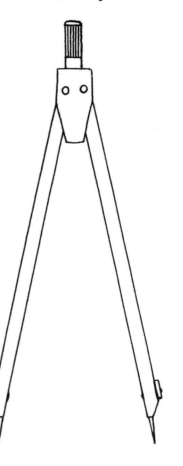

" x‐height" 5 n ws
rule space

nib widths

3x‐height

Five nib widths give the letter height of the letters x, o or i, called x‐height; set off this unit on the top line of the text; set the divi‐ders' legs 3 x‐heights apart; set one leg at the point that is the intersection of the line already ruled as the top line of the text block and the left hand, vertical margin; step off the spacing down the vertical length of the text area, say 18 times, a standard number of lines to a page of script. Do not press too hard: pressure can alter the span of the dividers. These light pricks are to mark the base line rules; to measure off the top of the x-height above each of the rules, step off the dividers from the top of the x-height on the top row. Provided the span of the dividers has not been altered at all, the result will be a series of points, in pairs, pricked down the left margin. With ruler parallel to the margin, and set square, rule the page.

Appendix

Ruling pen:

This, as the name implies, is a tool especially for ruling lines with ink. Ink may be applied with a dropper, or a brush. One drop is enough, and should be inserted between the blades of the nib. The screw controls the distance between the blade points, which determines line thickness: thinnest when closed, thicker when opened allowing a variety of effects. Provided the ink is contained within the blades, the pen nib may be drawn along the edge of a ruler, even a non-bevelled one, or a set square, with no smearing or running of ink.

Also, the ruling pen usually comes with a compasses in graphic art or drafting suppliers; the ruling pen nib is detachable from its handle, and can be interchanged with the pencil-lead attachment of the professional compasses. This makes it possible to draw perfect circles in ink, as in the geometrically drawn letters of the alphabet; by a combination of ruling pen for the straight lines, and compasses for the curves, the alphabet can be drawn entirely with tools, as we have seen, pp.104–145, above.

Appendix

Paper and Ink:

last but not least, for art and calligraphy good paper is necessary. You need some top grade paper, a few sheets of the best make available, for very special work. But for everyday work you need a stock of paper which need not be handmade, sized, deckle edged or watermarked. You can get a single-ply Bristol Board, acid-free or 'P-H neutral', with a high rag content, which is quite serviceable and takes Chinese (*non waterproof*), Indian (*waterproof*) black inks; Tempera, Gouache, or designers' colours. Spirit-based inks may bleed on single-ply Bristol, though, and watercolour wash cockles this paper.

The best ink is the stick sort, a little finger length of pressed carbon, bound in a med~ ium of gum. This has to be hand ground in a slate slab, available at the supplier. A few drops, less than half a teaspoon, in the grinding stone is sufficient to dissolve the stick into a strong, solid black; too much water takes too long to blacken, as even a few drops may need ten minutes to rub to jet blackness. Alternatively, Chinese (or Japanese) sumi ë ink comes in bottles, ready to use. Indian ink is like Chinese ink, but with lacquer added to make it water - proof. Chinese ink is kinder to nibs and brushes, and washes out when dry, be~ ing non~waterproof.

Appendix

While sumië ink is traditionally preferred by scribes, it is suitable for quill, or metal nib dip pens, but not for fountain pens. On the other hand, writing fluid for pens such as Osmiroid or Sheaffer, etc., which are commonly used by calligraphers, is generally either not light-fast, so the dye fades in sunlight, or is acidic, leaving an acid burn after the colour has faded; it also bleeds on paper where Chinese or Indian works fine.

Recently, a new fountain pen ink has been developed, Pelikan Fount India drawing ink for Fountain Pens..it is opaque, light fast, and waterproof, and seems less gummy than plain Indian ink.

PART TWO

CELTIC DESIGN

❖

KNOTWORK

Contents

[168]

Introduction

The idea behind this primer of knot-work is to publish fully, once and for all, the secret method of the scribes who created these ornaments, with special emphasis on the intelligible form language of the three grids and of the craft geometry used in building panels.

I support these ideas with reference to traditional sources, a variety of plaits and simple knots, and a study of spiral knots. As an appendix, I offer sixty original variations on the ubiquitous Triquetra knot, number 7, page 313. The book is meant to be used with a pencil and paper at hand. I hope readers will reproduce the designs themselves, and apply them.

Chapter 1
The
Three
Grids

IN knot design, the first and most im – portant thing to know is how to lay the grid of dots which determines the form of the resulting knot. To do this, it is necessary to analyse the dot grid of a knot into three classes of grid: first, THE PRIMARY GRID; second, THE SECONDARY GRID; third, THE TERTIARY GRID. Let us look now at a simple knot to see how it depends upon all three grids in its construction. The knot is the FOUNDATION KNOT. It looks like this:

The foundation knot.

fig. 1

Two-by-two Primary, Secondary, Tertiary
Dot Grids.

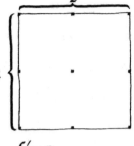

Primary is the square grid.
Each side of the square is
two squares. So the grid is
called a "2x2 Primary".

fig.2

Here we have the centres of
the squares. This grid is
a "2x2 Secondary" grid.
A "breakline" is placed between two secondary grid points.

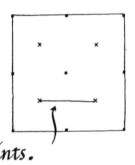

The 2x2 tertiary grid is
the path taken by the knot.
Each point on the tertiary
grid is the intersection
where the path crosses over
or under itself, except where cut by a breakline.

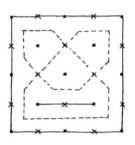

The combination grid.

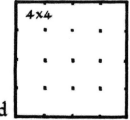

4x4

when you combine a 2x2
primary, secondary, &
tertiary, the result is a   d
4x4 primary. Compare this with the
grid on the previous page, fig.2. Can you
pick out the primary grid, 2x2, embedded
in the 4x4? The secondary? The tertiary?

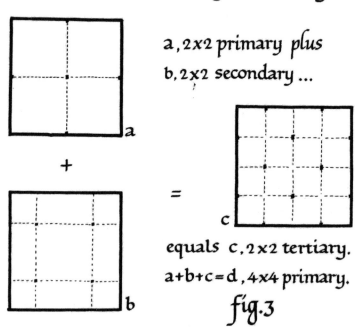

a, 2x2 primary plus
b, 2x2 secondary ...

a

+

=

b

c

equals c, 2x2 tertiary.
a+b+c=d, 4x4 primary.

fig.3

[172]

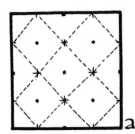

The breakline.

With no breakline, the
tertiary grid is a circuit
of a knot, or plaitwork.

The 2x2 square produces TWO links on
the tertiary grid. Can you see them in fig.4,
a?

In fig.4b you see the
line of the knot: it follows
the diamond pattern, tertiary grid.

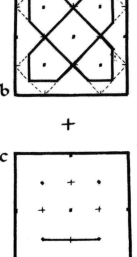

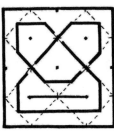

=   +

b, 2x2 plait plus
c, breakline equals d.

fig.4

[173]

 S we have seen, the Foundation Knot, *fig.1*, is derived from a grid, which may be seen as a combination of three distinct grids, which I call the primary, the secondary and the tertiary grid.

On page 171 we see the three grids in operation, building the knot through three stages. The primary grid divides the area into square spaces, so that we can call the knot a 2x2 knot. There are two spaces across and two down. In order to reproduce a knot design in the traditional way, it is first necessary to be able to count the spaces and then draw the primary dot grid. The primary grid here defines the outer edges. ▣

Counting from the corner of the box there are two primary cells a~long each edge, *fig*. 2. Each is a square, and the four cells meet in the centre. Each square has its own centre point, where lines joining opposite corners cross diagonally. The centre of the square is as obvious, as necessary as the centre of a circle. Every cell in the primary grid must have a centre point. Hence the secondary grid - the four centres form a single square cell over lapping, binding together the primary grid~rises spontaneously within the primary grid.

The primary grid and the second-ary grid intersect, unite to produce a third grid; again, spontaneously.

Chapter II
King
Solomon's
Knot

Compare *fig.3c* and *fig.4a*. You can see that by joining the tertiary grid points you get the form line of a 2x2 knot, which is the simplest on two accounts:

1, we cannot draw a square knot, or plait, on a grid less than 2x2;

2, there is no breakline in the 2x2 plait.

Knots are made with breaklines on the primary grid, or, as is the case with the Foundation Knot,

on the secondary grid, *fig.* 4 d . On
the other hand, plaitwork corresponds
to the diamond pattern of the tertiary grid, uninterrupted by any
breakline; *fig.* 4a, which illus~
trates the 2x2 plait perfectly,
raises one small problem. According to the definition we have just
made, it is clearly a plait; yet, at
least since Renaissance times, it
has been called 'King Solomon's Knot.'
In view of this, I will keep peace with
the tradition, and stick to the old
name. Intriguingly, it is said that
all the wisdom of Solomon is hidden in this knot. In a similar way,
the mediæval name for Solomon's
Knot, "The Emblem of Divine In~
scrutability", suggests that knots
were once contemplated as sym~

bols with religious or arcane philoso-
phical meanings.

For example, the way in which
the square, primary, and its centre,
secondary, provide the coordinates
for the division of the sides of the
square, tertiary, may have been
seen by early monks as a symbol
of tri-unity, three in one. The single square, 1x1 primary, spontaneously and simultaneously contains
a centre point, yet the square is a
unity, and the centre, 1x1 secondary,
is equally one in principle with the
square: they are as inseparable as
the circle and its centre. The centre
and the periphery of the square are
further related by the third, the
tertiary unit, the cross which passes

through the centre, the arms of which divide the sides of the square. So the wholeness of the unity is acted upon from within itself, by the action of its own centre, one divided by one, resulting in one. To the monks of early Christianity, the geometry of the square symbolized the creation of the manifold universe, and it was important to them to contemplate how the Two - the infinite and the finite, indeed all opposites - could be engendered by the One; the passage from One to Two must have been a reference of the symbol associated with 'Divine Inscrutability' and the epitome of wisdom, King Solomon. The passage from One to Two is symbolized by the grid: 1x1 primary, secondary, tertiary = 2x2.

fig. 5   The Three Grids of a Square.

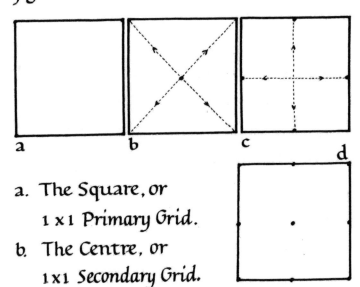

a.   The Square, or
  1 x 1 Primary Grid.

b.   The Centre, or
  1 x 1 Secondary Grid.

c.   The Mid-points of the Sides or
  1 x 1 Tertiary Grid.

d.   The Tri-une, or Combination 1 x 1,
  is <u>at the same time</u> a 2 x 2 primary,
  symbolizing passage from One to Two,
  while also symbolizing the Three-in-
  One.

fig. 6   The Development of the 2x2 Grid.

a. 1x1 Primary Grid.
The Primary Grid is
the *first step* in the development of any knot   a
or plait: it defines the
corners of the square
area to be decorated.
Here, the square symbo-
lizes unity, origination.   b

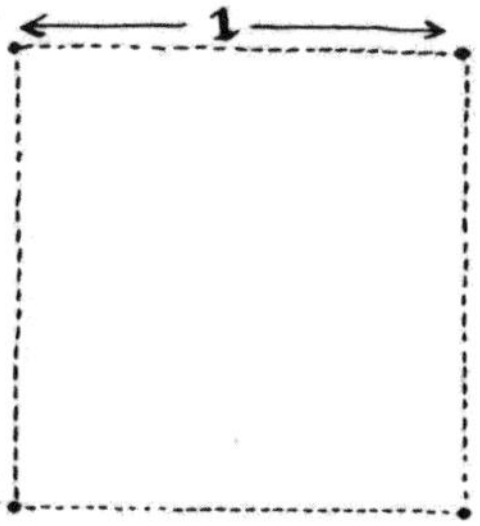

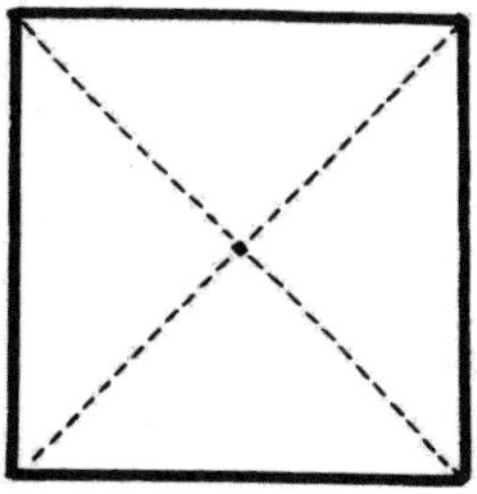

c

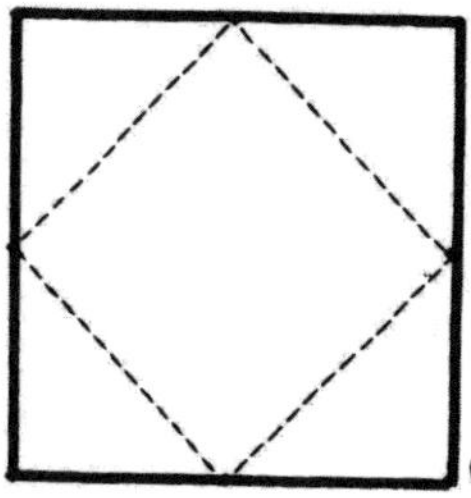

d

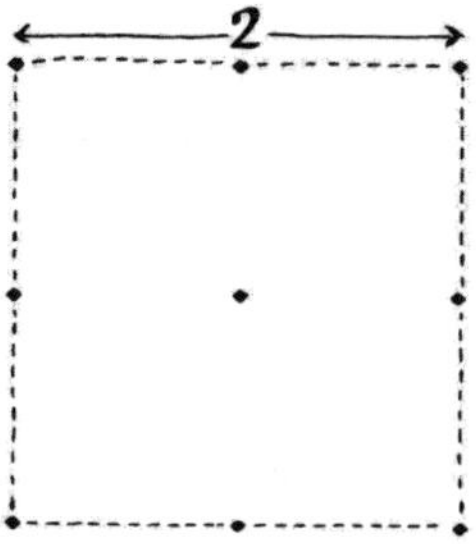

b. 1x1 Diagonal Cross, Secondary Grid: Centre.
c. 1x1 Tertiary Grid; Diamond : Turning Square.
d. Three grids together produce 2x2 Primary.

[181]

fig.7 The 2×2 Grids; Primary, Secondary, & Tertiary.

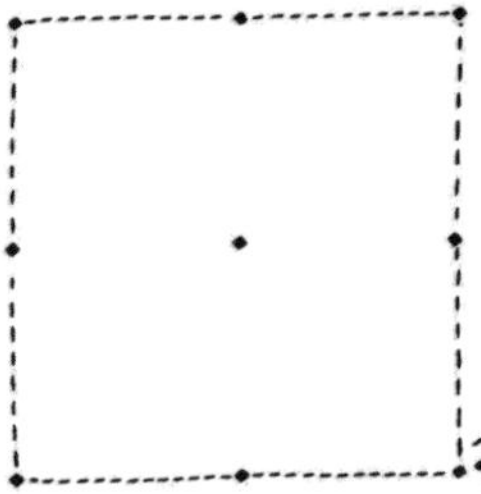

a 2×2 Primary dot grid

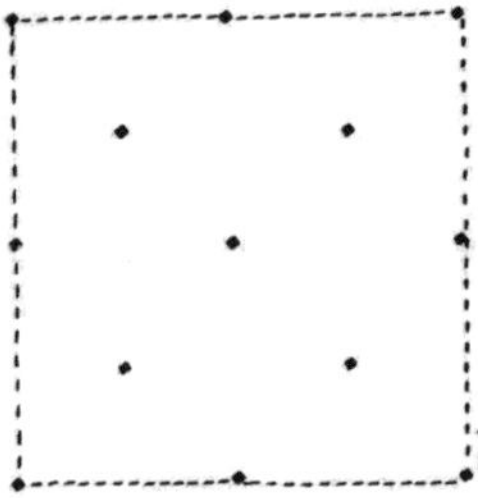

2 × 2 Primary dot grid
plus
b 2×2 Secondary dot grid

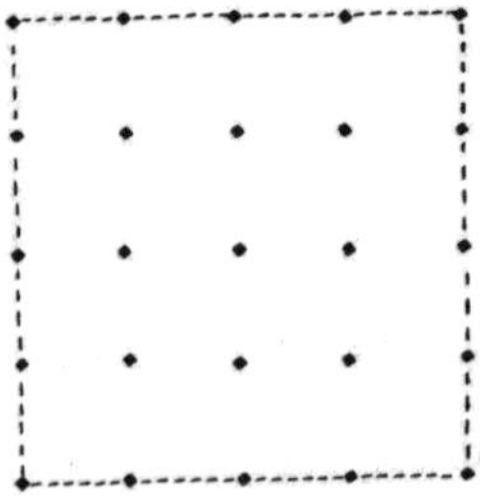

2×2 Primary dot grid
plus
2 × 2 Secondary dot grid
plus
c 2×2 Tertiary dot grid

fig. 8 Weaving the Line on the Tertiary Grid.

a. The tertiary grid
forms a diamond pattern;
there are 4 intersections,
each a tertiary grid dot. a.

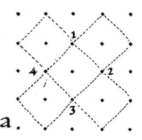

b. Start in the corner, a
line section from centre
to centre on the combina-
tion grid ~*fig.*7c~ this   b
gives the unit gap.

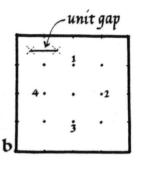

c. Continue the line
through the first tertiary
grid dot. Stop short of
the second tertiary grid   c
dot, leaving a space equal to the unit gap.

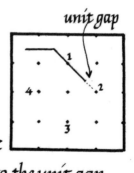

fig.8 : continued...

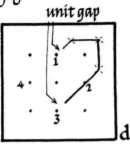

d. Start at 1, leave unit gap; turn corner; pass through intersection 2.

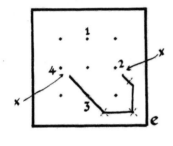

e. From under 2, leave gap; turn corner; pass through intersection.

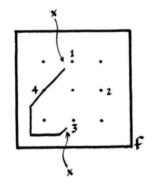

f. The final corner turn.

fig.9 The four corner turns, in sequence.

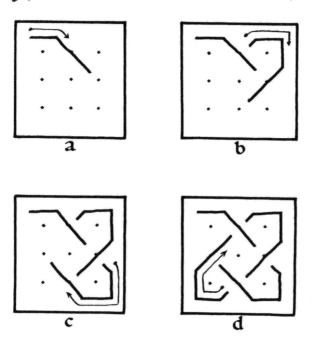

a   b

c   d

The lines of this design may be drawn in order, clockwise. Do not forget the final touch, e.

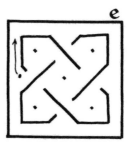

e

fig.10 Outline the woven line

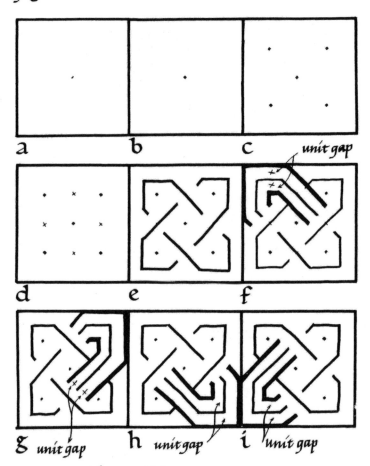

a–d. The grid layout.

e. The woven line.

f–i. Outlines either side of woven line.

fig. 11   Filling the Background.

a   b

a.   King Solomon's Knot, woven centre-line of the knot has been outlined segment by segment.

b.   The background has been inked in. This completes King Solomon's Knot.
    Notice that the grid points have all disappeared into the background of the knot.

    The end result is a broad-ribbon treatment. The ribbon width here is as wide as it properly should be, based on the maximum unit gap.

chapter III
the
foundation
knot

HE FOUNDATION KNOT
derives from Solomon's
Knot. As Solomon's Knot
is actually the simplest form of regular plaitwork, having a 2x2 grid base,
the Foundation Knot is the simplest
regular knot: the only regular knot
that can be obtained from the 2x2 grid.
So, it provides an example of how
knotwork is derived from plaitwork,
and for one who has followed the method of drawing Solomon's Knot so

far, the Foundation Knot will be easy to
master as it has so many steps in common with Solomon's.

The following figures show how to
draw the Foundation Knot; all you
need to draw with is a pen and paper,
no need to pencil sketch or erase. Start
big, with a square about the size of
the palm of your hand. Then, each
time you repeat the exercise, start
smaller, till you can draw the knot
the size of your little finger nail, or
as small as your pen or eye allows.

fig. 12 The Foundation Knot.

fig.13 Foundation Knot Construction

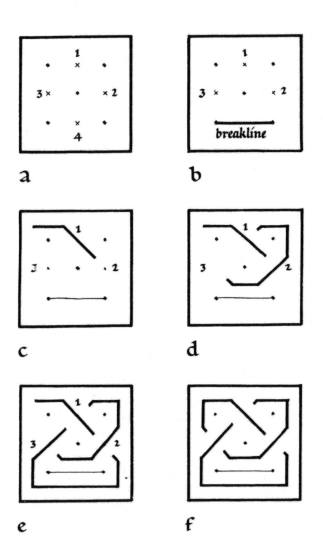

a

b

breakline

c

d

e

f

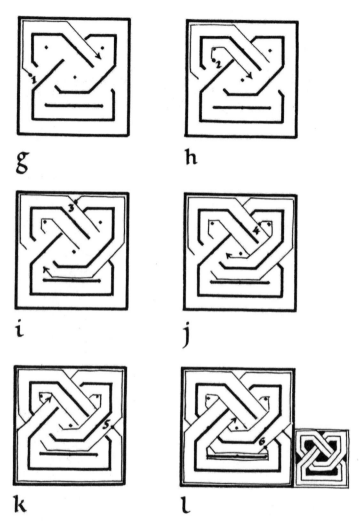

g

h

i

j

k

l

Outline each of the three line segments
with two outlines at a time, every time.

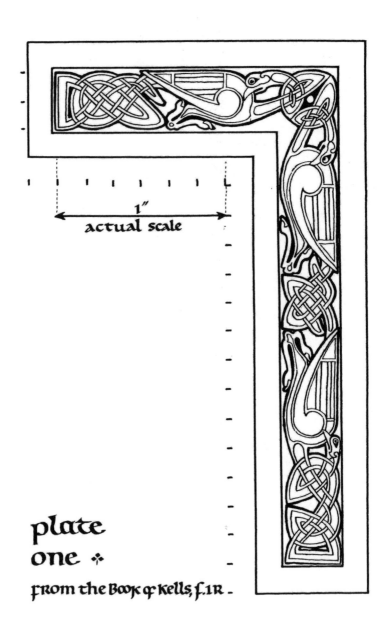

1"
actual scale

plate
one ❖
from the Book of Kells, f.1R

[192]

chapter IV
Extending
Knots & the
Josephine Knot

ING Solomon's Knot oc‒
cupies a square contain-
ing a dot grid 2 units
across and 2 down. To extend this
knot, let us first double it. Two u-
nits will fill a box containing four
spaces across and two down, that is,
a 4 x 2 dot grid. The result is what
I call 4x2 plait. Its construction is
illustrated in the following figures.

fig. 14. Extending the grid to 4x2.

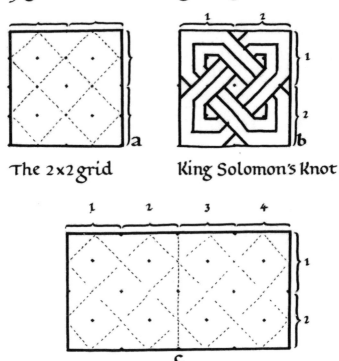

The 2x2 grid

King Solomon's Knot

The 4x2 grid

As you can see by comparing the grids at a and c, the 4x2 grid is double the 2x2.

Two 2x2's placed side by side make up the 4x2

2 x 2 + 2 x 2 = 4 x 2

fig. 15   The 4×2 Plait Construction

2×1 Primary Grid
   two squares

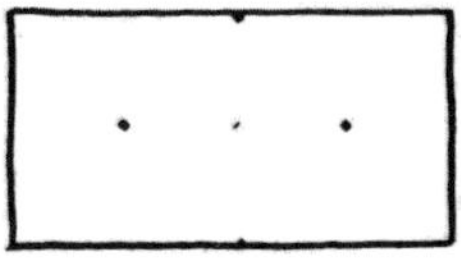

2×1 Secondary
   two mid-points

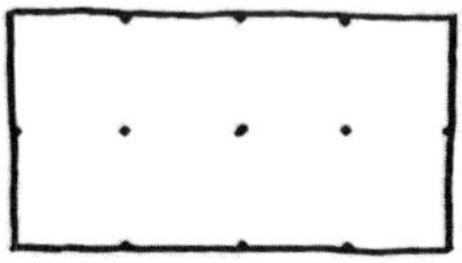

2×1 Pri., sec.,& ter.,
= 4×2 pri.

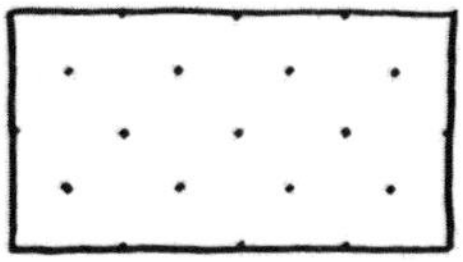

4 x 2 pri.& sec.

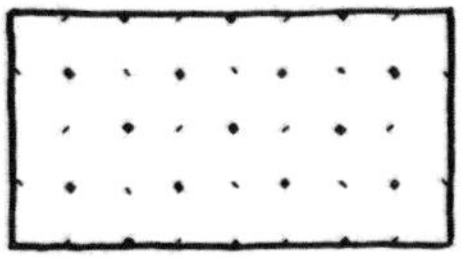

4×2 pri.& sec. & ter.

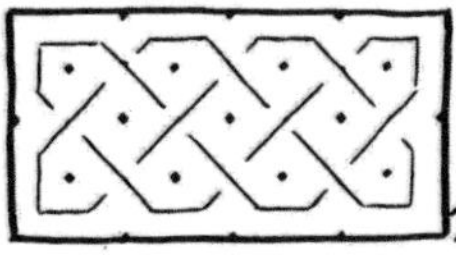

The 4x2 Tertiary Grid
provides the crossover
points for weaving.

[195]

fig. 15 , continued.

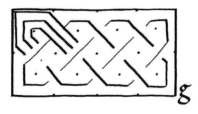

g

Outline each line
segment with a
double outline

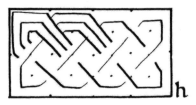

h

i

j

Fill in the back-
ground.

This design was drawn entirely with an
italic nib, and Indian ink, and ruler edge.

[196]

**ust as** the Four-by-Two Plait may be viewed as a pair of Solomon's Knots side by side, so a pair of Foundation Knots may be made into a Four-by-two Knot, fig. 16.

fig. 16   The Four-by-Two Knot

The larger dots are primary & secondary. Break lines go on Sec. grid.

a

Compare with fig. 15, f.

b

d   **c**

fig. 17. Josephine Knot.

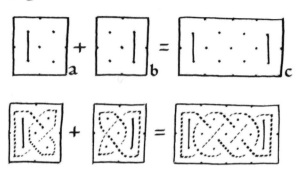

As here, the Foundation Knot may be turned sideways, a & b, using vertical breaklines; when these two breaks are put into the 4x2 grid, as here, c, the result is the Josephine Knot.

OSEPHINE was Napoleon Bonaparte's empress, and was a favorite of the seamen of those days, or so we might guess, for this is a knot that is traditional to sailors. It is also a Celtic knot that

was popular over a thousand years ago, and still is, among Celtic artists.

The Josephine Knot is also a lover's knot. Two intertwined links make this whole pattern.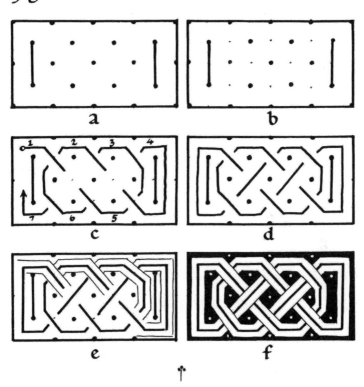

fig.18   Construction of Josephine Knot.

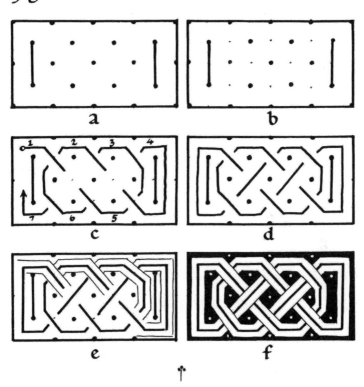

a

b

c

d

e

f

fig. 19 Repeat border of Josephine Knots

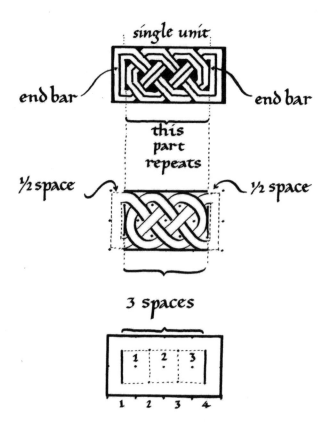

single unit

end bar   end bar

this part repeats

½ space   ½ space

3 spaces

1   2   3

1   2   3   4

Josephine's knot is actually three spaces wide, on the secondary grid, if you count between the breaklines. The single unit has two bars splicing together the loose ends.

fig. 20 Josephine Knot border, 2 units.

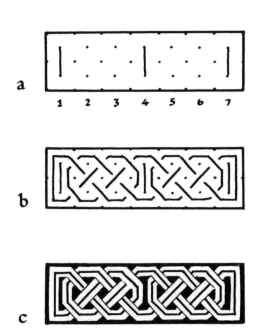

a

1 2 3 4 5 6 7

b

c

The repeat is 3 spaces, 2 units is 6.
To close the ends, ½ space at either end.
Thus, total of spaces for 2 units is 7.
— here, 3 N + 1 (where N = 2) = 7 —
The rule is: (the number of spaces to a repeat)
by N (the number of repeats) plus 1 (½ + ½).

[201]

fig. 21 Josephine Knot Border, 3 units.

Q. How many spaces are required to fit 3 units of Josephine's Knot?

A. Let N equal the number of repeats required, then N = 3.

Let X equal the number of spaces required by the repeating part of the knot.

Since the single unit requires bars, one at each end, and each one is ½ a space, then the border will need XN+1 spaces all told.

X = 3 ; N = 3 . Therefore XN+1 = 10.
10 spaces are required by a 3 unit border of Josephine Knots.

[202]

fig. 21 , continued...

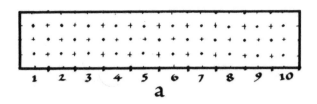

a

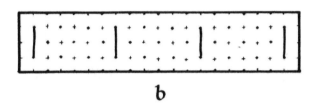

b

c

a & b laid out on a ruled square grid
with medium italic nib in holder.
c drawn directly on grid b; centre line
"Speedball B4" nib; outline, "Speedball FB6."

[203]

fig. 22 Ten Square Panel of Josephine's Knots

The background is left open so you can see the construction of primary & secondary grid dots, & breaklines.

chapter v
Building
a panel

MALL KNOTS are easily done on a freehand drawn dot grid, but for a larger panel, or where accuracy is desired, a geometric layout is good to know how to do. We have been accustomed to a square grid, divided in two, four, eight, etc. We can divide a line in two, surely, by eye. So we can build an accurate grid by halfing, quartering and so on indefinitely. But a five-fold grid is another matter. It is not so easy to draw a five-by-five grid on large scale, by eye. There is a simple method from the Book of Lindisfarne, however, by which a five-square grid may be produced, using traditional geometry.

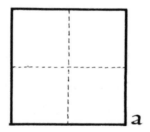

fig. 23   Construction of Octagon Star in
Square

Given:

a square divided into 4. Find the centre first, then divide the sides...

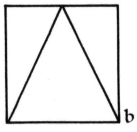

With a pencil, join the midpoint of one side to opposite corners.

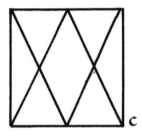

Repeat from the opposite side.

Complete on all sides.

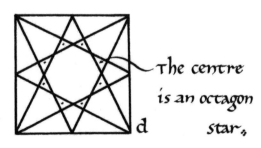

The centre is an octagon star.

fig. 24 Derivation of Five-fold Grid from Octagon Star.

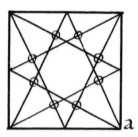

a

These eight points, when joined, divide the square into five, thus:

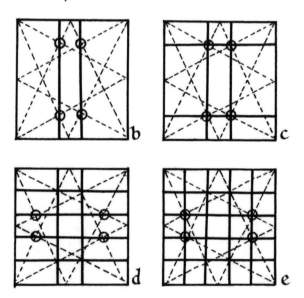

b

c

d

e

fig.25.   Doubling the Five-by-Five Grid
         by means of the Octagon Star.

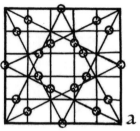

a

These twenty points split the 5²grid into
a 10²grid. Note: compare with *fig*.24,*e*.
The star that produces the 5²also cuts it
at the points which produce the 10², *f*.25,*a*.

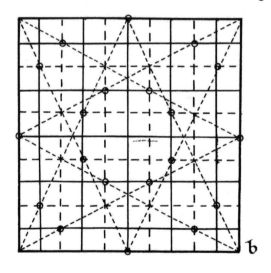

b

[209]

fig. 26   Derivation of 10² by Octagon Star
& 2² Diagonal Grid

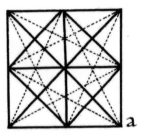

a: the 2² diagonal grid, (and the 2² primary).

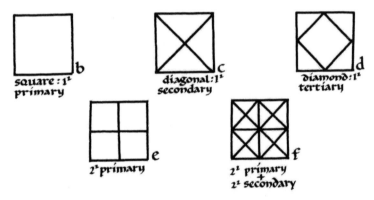

1²primary. b, + 1²secondary, c, + 1²tertiary, d

= 2²primary. e.   Combined b,c,d,e =f.

f may also be read as 2² primary + secondary.

Square = prim., Diagonal = sec., Diamond = tert.

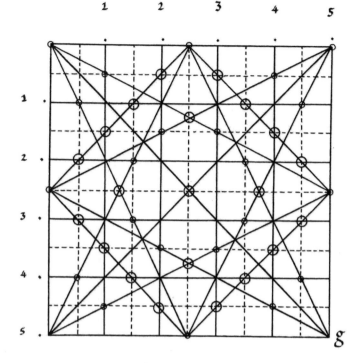

g

The 2x2 grid at a, opposite page, is already
implied in the diagonal, vertical & horizontal
axes of the octagon star. The star produces a
5x5 grid, f.24, and splits this into 10x10.
By using the 2^2 grid, f.26a, we generate so
many more divisions of the 5x5 grid that
the 10^2 may be ruled with more precision.

fig. 27. Five-squared dot grids.

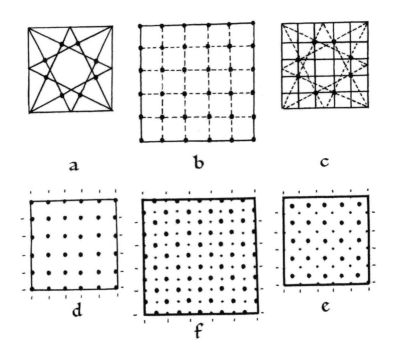

a   b   c

d   f   e

using the star, a, produce a 5^2 grid. A
sharp, hard pencil - 6H - is ideal. On the pencilled grid, b, ink the square dot grid, d;
that is the 5^2 primary. Mark in ink the centre
of each cell, e; 5^2 secondary. Ink the tertiary, f.

[212]

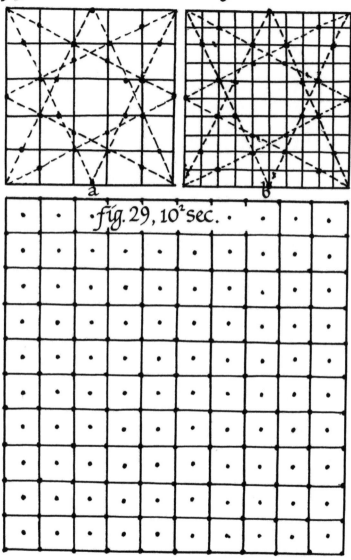

fig.28 a,b , 10² from Octagon Star

fig. 29, 10² sec.

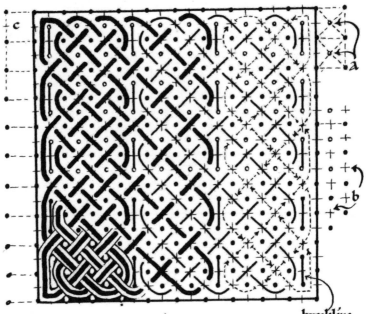

breakline

fig. 30 Construction for Fig. 22.

On the 10² secondary grid are placed the
breaklines for the pattern.

Next, pencil the tertiary grid, here marked
as crosses, b.

Now weave the line of the knot, passing over
& under the intersection points, i.e. the
pencilled tertiary grid. Note: the primary
counts the spaces; secondary=breaks; tert.=knot.

[214]

fig. 31 Construction of panel, fig. 32,
10² panel of Josephine Knots, variation no. 2.
variation no. 1, page 204.

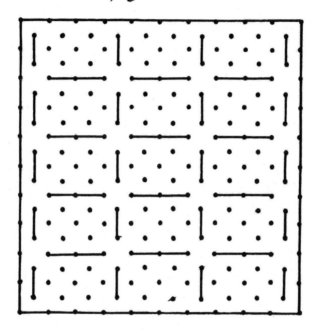

Here the vertical breaklines, on the secondary
grid, are the same as on opposite page. However,
breaklines may be laid on the primary grid, to
distinguish units of repeat patterns, as is
the case here: horizontal breaks on primary ...

fig 32   A.M. June 5 '86┼

chapter VI
Analysis of
plaitwork

 N REPEATING a
knot we use
each of the three grids
in different ways.
So, a border of Josephine knots, p.203,
involves counting separate spacings
on the secondary & primary grids.
   A border of Josephines involving
the formula on p. 202 is obvious at a
glance as a series of units. But in
the vertical repeat of the border –
p.204– the knot is lost.

The knot unit in horizontal repeat
is defined well enough by the breaks
on the secondary grid, but to keep it
as well defined in a panel, as on p. 216,
we must use primary grid, horizontal breaks, p. 215. This shows the impor-
tance of being able to distinguish between one dot and another. Take, for
example, the square dot grid on p. 220,
f. 34, c. Pick any dot on the 5^2 combination and see if you can tell if it
is a primary, secondary or tertiary
grid dot. If you have been following
the figures to this point, you will be
able to do this.

You will also have realised that
when drawing the lines of the inter-
lace, the tertiary grid dots become
intersection points which are swal-
lowed by the cross over, f. 33, a.

fig. 33 Three Grid & Two Grid method.

three grid method.   a

two grid method.   b

However, this method requires a
centreline thicker than the tertiary
dot, or the dot will show through,
and spoil the appearance. It is better
to draw the line by the two grid method, to learn to see the path of the
tertiary grid as the white path between the domino-spots of the
primary-secondary dot grid.

fig.34 Corner turn & Edge bend

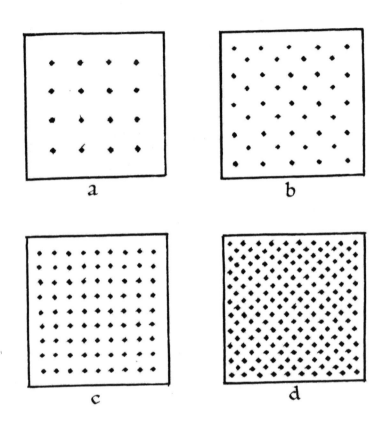

a

b

c

d

a : five by five primary dot grid.

b : five by five secondary dot grid
plus five by five primary dot grid.

c: five by five primary dot grid, plus
five by five secondary dot grid, plus
five by five tertiary...

which is also
ten by ten primary dot grid.

This ten by ten square grid of dots now
becomes the basis of the next stage...
d: ten by ten primary dot grid plus
ten by ten secondary dot grid.

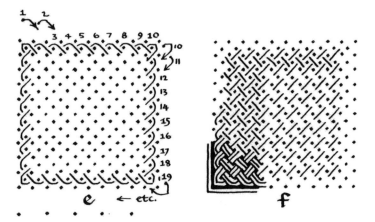

e: weave the centre line thus.
f: complete weave; outline; fill in.

fig.35 Five by Five Plaitwork Panel

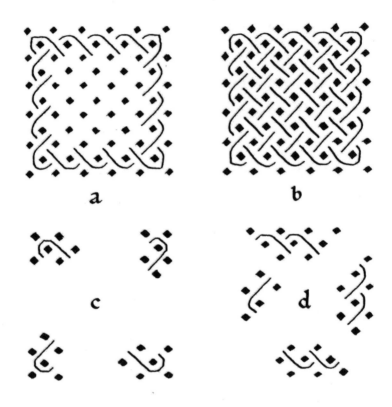

a   b

c   d

a. Weaving the corners and edges.
b. Weaving the straight strands.
c. The four corner elements.
d. The four side-edge elements.

fig.36 Chequer Effect of straight strands.

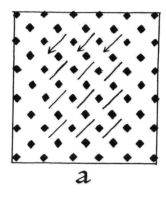

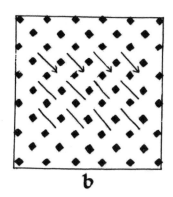

a   b

Straight strokes cross diamonds:
a. Straight strokes, right to left.
b. Straight strokes, left to right.
c,d Strokes correspond to chequer.

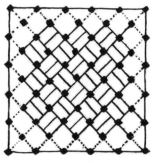

d   the grid forms a   c chequer board

fig.37 First stroke-corner Triangle & Diamond

a   b

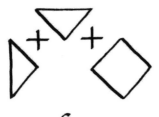

c

the corner is composed of two triangles & a diamond.

second stroke, edge Bend :

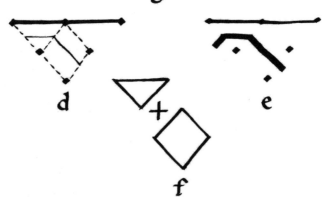

d   f   e

the edge is one triangle & one diamond.

fig. 38 Second Stroke, Edge Triangle & Diamond

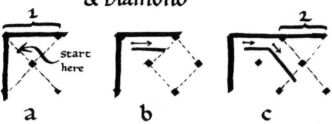

a   b   c

Starting at the top right-hand corner, on the diagonal axis, a; cross the triangle, b. This cuts the side common to both triangle & diamond. The next move is to cross the diamond. Start the second stroke in tri-

~ remaining edge strokes ~

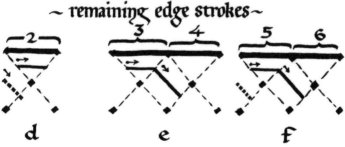

d   e   f

angle 2, d; repeat stroke to left ~

hand corner. Note the triangle is one space, or primary grid unit along the edge. The corner at top right of the 10^2 plait will be the tenth triangle. Along the edge, each stroke passes through a triangle, turns around the secondary grid point & through the diamond. This holds true for all edge bends. The corner turn, however, differs from that again, for it involves two triangles.

fig.39

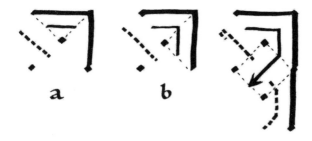

a   b   c

fig 40 Diagonal Opposition of
Straight Strokes.

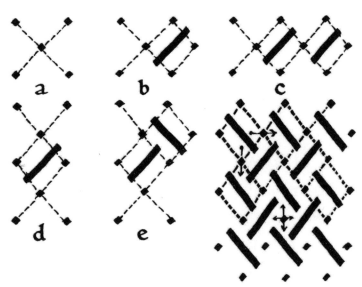

a b c

d e

the diamonds point-to-   f
point, across, c, or down, d,
are identical.

Diamonds side-to-side are opposed, on the diagonal directions,
e. You cannot cross more than
one diamond at a time (in any
direction.

At this stage, we continue to use the tertiary grid in the build up of the dot grid. However, we will only use the primary and secondary grid for the interlacing, p. 219. This is a new method, and so it has been introduced in the present analysis of plaitwork, to practise drawing plaitwork without drawing the tertiary grid intersection points at all. As we shall see later, once you can do this, it will be possible to explore a variety of treatments of plaits and knots, by the two-grid method.

With this method our perception changes from one of connecting dots to one of dividing triangles and diamonds: the dividing of surface by line.

fig 41 square plait, Dot & line

a. 2 x 2 square plait.

    ❖

⤶ two links.

b. 3 x 3 square plait.

    ❖

⤶ three links.

c. 4 x 4 square plait.

    ❖

⤶ four links.

d. 5x5 square plait.
⤶ count the links. d

fig. 42 square plait; outline & fill in.

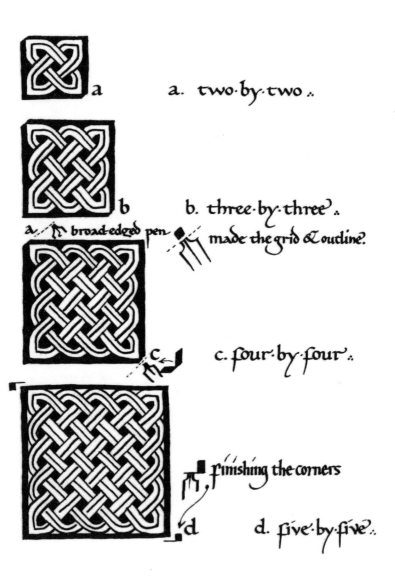

a. two·by·two ..

b. three·by·three ..

a. ↑ broad-edged pen made the grid & outline.

c. four·by·four ..

finishing the corners

d. five·by·five ..

chapter VII
plaitwork
to practise

 LAITWORK as well
as knotwork may
be continuous or
discontinuous; that is, made up
of a single, continuous, endless
path, or of more than one path,
several interlinked circuits.
Square plaits have as many links
as spaces along the side, figs.41,42.
Add a row, and the plait becomes a

fig. 43 Rectangular plait: dot & line

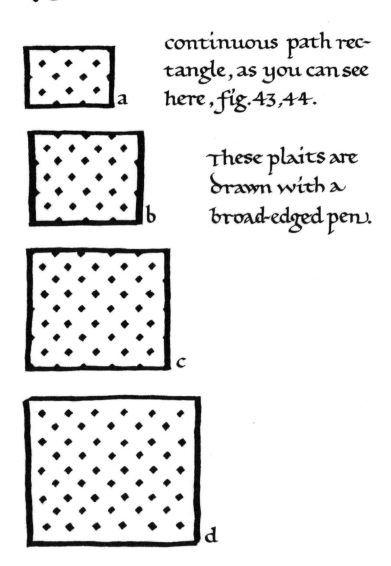

continuous path rec-
tangle, as you can see
here, fig. 43, 44.

These plaits are
drawn with a
broad-edged pen.

fig. 44 Rectangular plait: Outline & fill

a

b

The rule is:
numbers with
no common
factor produce
an endless line
plait.

c

a: 3×2 ; b: 4×3;
c: 5×4; d: 6×5. d

fig.45 10² Cross: Primary Grid

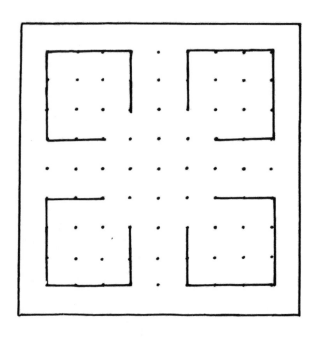

The Cross
Panel

fig.46   10² cross : secondary Grid

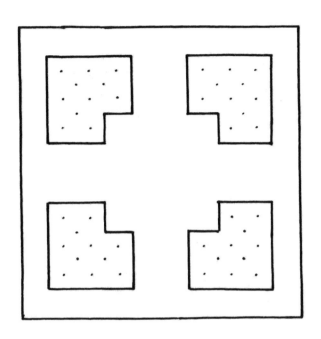

Carpet-Page design

figs. 46 – 51.

fig.47 10² cross ∴ background panels

A show piece of the art of decoration, the Carpet-page design,
so-called by virtue of its resemblance
to the design of a persian carpet, often

[236]

fig.48 10² Cross · Foreground

takes the form of a cross panel in the
decorated Gospel books such as Durrow,
Lichfield (a.k.a Chad), Lindisfarne &
Kells. In Durrow, plaitwork is used
to decorate the panel.

fig.49 20² Cross: primary grid

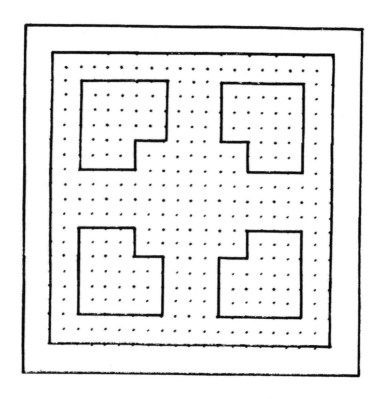

Figs. 45,46,47,48: a simple exercise, a 10² cross with plaitwork inlaid background, 47, or reverse form, 48; to combine both forms, a separating band or

fig. 50 20² Cross: Secondary Grid

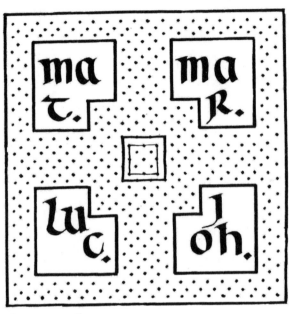

Background: mat(theus), mar(cus), luc(as), io(han) fillet is called for, requiring a 20²grid–obtained from the 10²array– 49, 50.f.

In fig. 51, overleaf, the background knots are fillet-bound.

fig.51   Twenty square plaitwork Cross;

drawn with Canada Goose quill.

Aidan
June 9 '86

[240]

chapter VIII
Division of
a square

quills & lampblack ink +

HE GREAT FULL-LENGTH
decorated pages are
constructed on grids
built geometrically,
based on a square. The first step is
to divide the square. Two ways are
shown, figs. 55 & 56. The latter follows
more directly from the construction of a
square, fig. 53, though both are canonical.
Less satisfactory, because less symbolical-
ly intelligible, therefore non-canonical,
is fig. 54, though it is a sensible method.

[241]

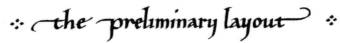

fig. 52 ✠ Cross Panel of St. Chad ✠

❖ the preliminary layout ❖

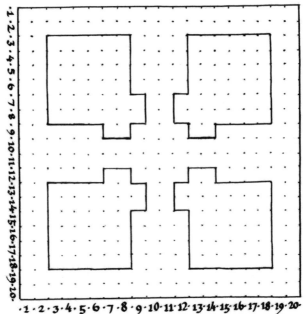

·1·2·3·4·5·6·7·8·9·10·11·12·13·14·15·16·17·18·19·20·

20² primary dot grid.　　　　~ layout of fig. 51.

❖

To construct the grid using the traditional method, compasses & straight edge a-
lone, begin with a square, fig. 52, and
then a 5² grid, as at fig. 24.

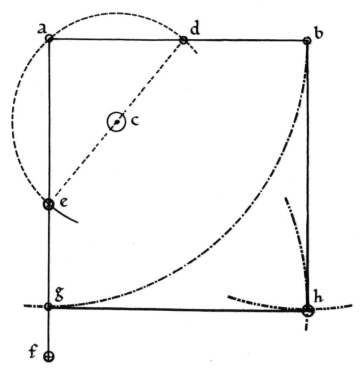

fig. 53 Canonical Construction of the Square ❖

Given a length, ab, to be the side of the
square, place point of compasses below
the line ab, and with radius ac, cut ab at
point d. Join d through c to cut the
curve at e. Produce perpendicular to f.

[243]

fig.53, continued:

Having produced the corner, baf, now describe the arc, radius ab, cutting af at g.

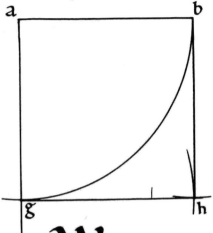

With centres b. and g, draw a pair of arcs of radius ab, cutting one another at h.

This done, rule up the square, abhg, in ink, and erase the fine-pencilled cons-truction.

The next step is to produce the ver-tical cross, the Trinity Grid, f. 3a, p. 172.

fig. 54 The Quartering of the Square, by the vertical cross.

Find the centre of the square, by means of the diagonal cross, e.

With centres c, d, radius c,e, produce the arcs ef.

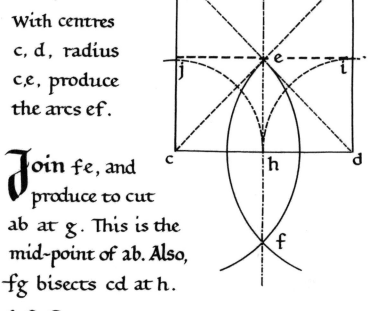

Join fe, and produce to cut ab at g. This is the mid-point of ab. Also, fg bisects cd at h.

With centres cd, radius ch, produce arcs to bisect ac at j, and bd at i. Thus is the vertical cross made.

fig. 55 The Division of the Square: Canonical :: Method ::

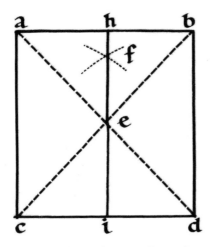

As the line **ab** is the unit with which we begin, we can best demonstrate the division of unity by unity thus: let the line **ab** be 1, then the square is 1x1, which is one. Now the divis- of the square is accomplished within the square by the diagonal **ad** or **bc**, so that **abc** equals **dcb**.

While this divides the unity of the square, it does not di-

vide the side; to achieve the division
of side by diagonal, as f.54, takes us outside the square. The method here is canonical, simpler, internal; the sides
are used to divide the sides themselves,
$1 \div 1 = 1$, thus main-
taining unity.

fig.55:
centres **c,d,**
rad.**ca**, find **f**;
join **ef**, and
produce to **h,i**

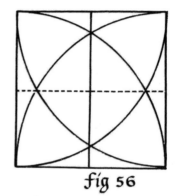

fig 56

This method uses the sides and diagonals. Fig. 56 uses sides as radii only to
divide the square. Also, it establishes
the centre in a way that uses only
the square, rather than diagonal cross.
Both methods are canonical symbols
of the division of Unity, the Primal
Act of the Principle of Creation.

[247]

G iven the 2^2, we construct a 5^2, which splits into 10^2; divide and quarter this, i.e. 10^2 primary, secondary and tertiary, to arrive at the 20^2, and hence lay out the grid for the cross. Now we are ready to decorate the panel : first with plaitwork, as in fig. 57.

fig. 57 3^2 Knot as Panel :

$6^2 = 3^2$ PRI.   ♦

+ 3^2 SEC.   ■

+ 3^2 TER: -┼-

The panel is a square, 6^2 on the 20^2, 3^2~ pri, sec, ter-on the 10^2. Obviously, the 3^2 does not fit, being truncated.*

fig. 58   6² knot as Panel :

You can deduce from this plan that the square knot is a symmetrical pattern; in fact, continu-

ous. But, with the fishtail stepped onto the corner, a break may be dropped and continuity be preserved; either way is acceptable. Engineering a continuous path is a challenge of skill, though. This one will fit Chad's Cross.

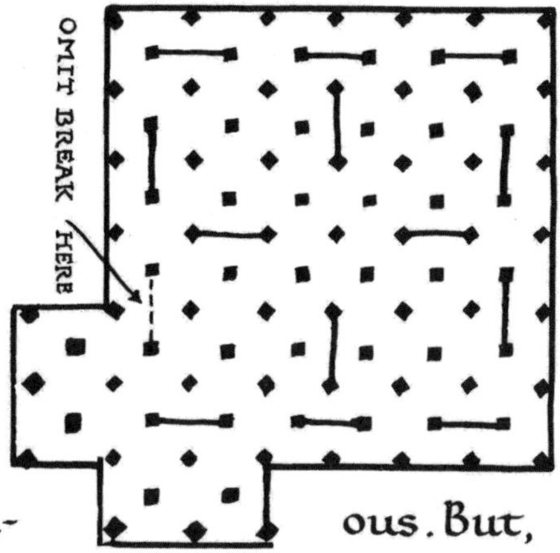

original design,
✝ ΛΛ'86

fig. 59   Full-length Carpet-page

Knot panels based on fig. 58 ∴
With or without breakline omission,
fig. 58 is continuous. The panel at
lower left uses all the breaks.

fig. 60 : Two Plans :

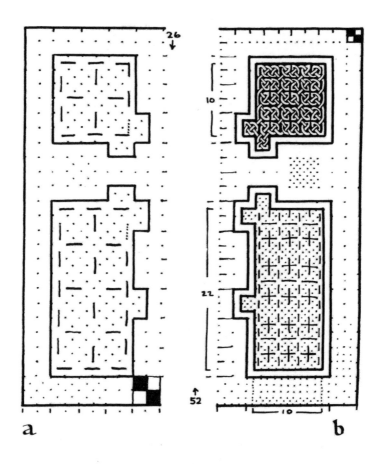

a: Plan of fig. 59.
b: Plan of fig. 61.

fig.61 Cross Carpet-page : 32x44 grid†

steel nibs & gouache black .

mcmlxxxvi.vi.xv.

Aidan †

chapter ix
plaitwork panel
from the
book of durrow

URROW is the earliest
of the fully illumin-
ated Gospel Books of
Celtic Art. Of special
interest is the open-
ing page, folio 1v, the carpet page with
two-armed cross. The cross-panel,
framed in knots, is itself inlaid with
plaitwork; i.e., it has no breaklines,
though crosslet inserts break the plaitwork. let us examine this great design

fig. 62   Crosslet Diaper: 18 x 24 grid

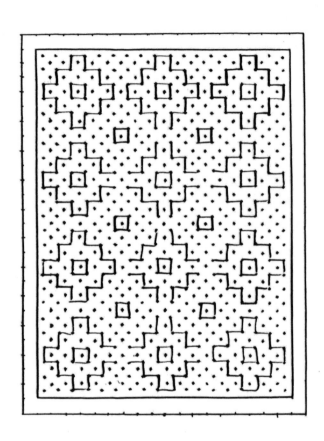

fig. 63   Double-Cross from Diaper

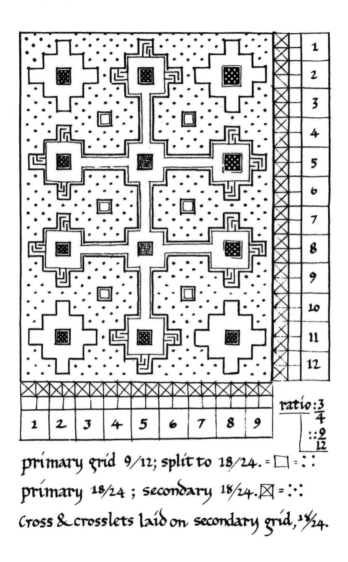

primary grid 9/12; split to 18/24. = □ = ∴

primary 18/24 ; secondary 18/24. ⊠ = ∴

Cross & crosslets laid on secondary grid, 18/24.

[255]

fig. 64 Celtic Crosslet : Knot & Spiral :

the crosslet is on a smaller grid than
the surrounding knot. The crosslet
knot construction is shown on
page 261, f. 70.

fig. 65 : Crosslet with key pattern :

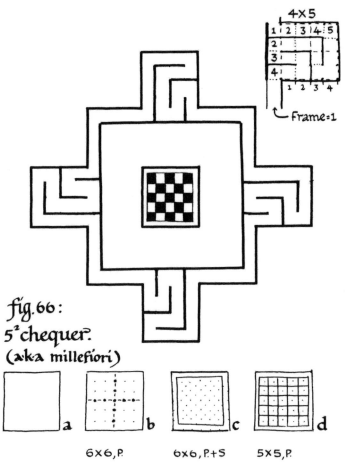

4×5

	1	2	3	4	5
2					
3					
4					

1   2   3   4

Frame=1

fig. 66 :
5² chequer.
(aka millefiori)

a

b
6×6, P.

c
6×6, P.+S

d
5×5, P.

The centre chequer is a 5², surrounded
by a frame ½² wide; i.e., 5² primary, 6² secondary.

[257]

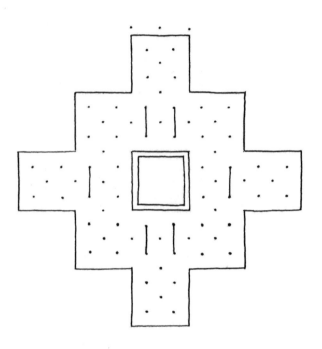

fig. 67 : Knotwork Crosslet : breakplan

fig. 68 : Knotwork Crosslet.

<—— 1/2" ——>

ACTUAL
SCALE
3/12"

The knot is not continuous.

fig. 69 : Swastika~Tau~Fret: Square:

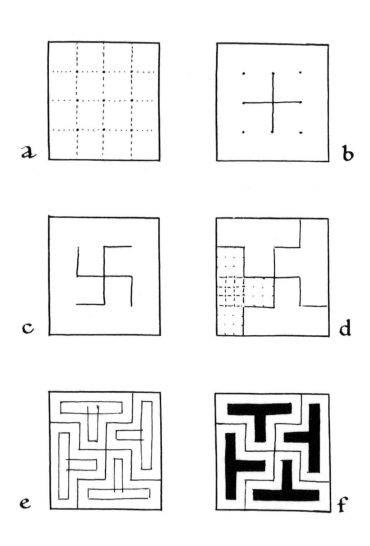

fig. 70 : knot & spiral construction of crosslet, fig. 64.

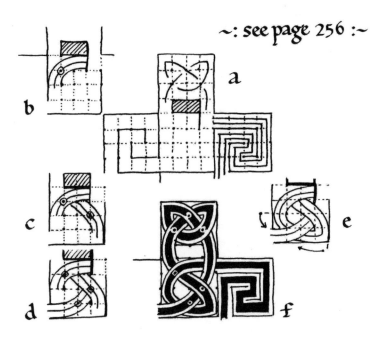

~: see page 256 :~

This is a combination of two knots, a regular Foundation Knot, a, and an irregular knot, b~e, separated by a box break, shaded. The odd knot crosses on a secondary grid dot, b.

[261]

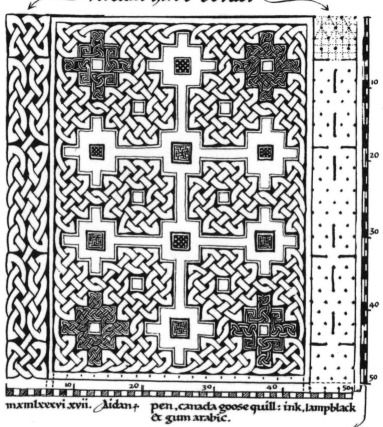

fig. 71 Durrow Cross Panel :
vertical knot border

mxmlxxxvi xvii. Aidan+   pen, canada goose quill : ink, lampblack
                                     & gum arabic.

(compress unavoidable extra space to fit 50^2)

Compare the cross panel above with plan on p. 255.
On the right here is the breakplan for the knot
strip to the left. The whole design fits a 50^2 grid.

[262]

fig.72   Step pattern from Sutton Hoo.

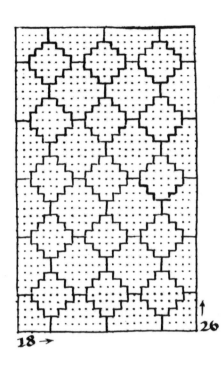

This pattern from the Saxon Ship Burial of Sutton Hoo. England may be the source of the Durrow carpet page. The resemblance is more than superficial. If the step pattern be outlined on the secondary grid. the resultant cells conform exactly to the grids required for the Durrow crosslets, see f. 62,63,71,73.

[263]

fig. 73　Sutton Hoo & Durrow in combination.

Both the Durrow crosslets fit the step pattern on the secondary grid.

The edge of this panel is 18 spaces. This is the primary grid, on which is laid a portion of the Sutton Hoo step pattern, page 263. The step pattern outlined & inlined on the secondary gives Durrow.

chapter x
spiral knots

PIRAL knots turn up here and there in knot designs in Celtic manuscripts, carved stones, and metal work. Usually they have been explained as being e-volved from putting a circle on a diagonal cross, or concentric circles on parallel diagonals, and breaking the circle to join a diagonal. Over leaf, you can see a spiral knot produced in that way.

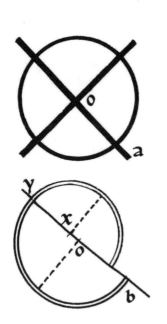

fig . 74   Spiral Knot;
          line method.

a. Wheel cross: circle
   & diagonals of a
   square.

b. Spiral: 2 semi-
   circles, centres O,x;
   joined at y.

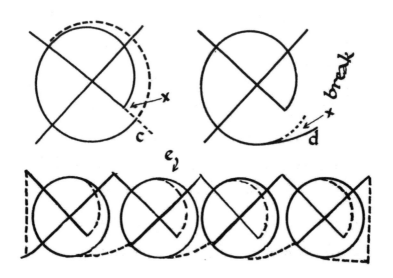

fig. 75 spiral knot: single unit to fill a square; pencil-erase method.

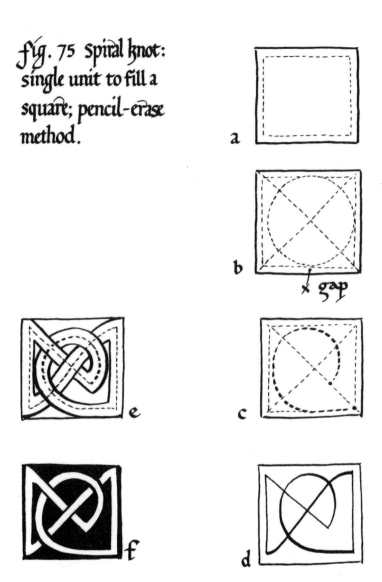

a

b

× gap

e

c

f

d

Pencil, a–d ; ink weave, e ; erase pencil, f.

fig. 76   Spiral knot ~ Four unit Border:

a. Draw the line of the knot in pencil :

See fig. 74.

b. Outline in pencil.

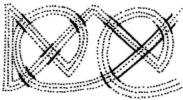

c. Mark crossover & under, define weave.

d. Outline the knot in ink; erase pencil.

fig. 77 Spiral knots; 2 Units, mirrored;

a. Pencil triple-line. b. Swastika crosses.

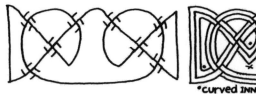

*curved INNER ✕ Point OUTER

c. Centre line, ink. d. Swastikas lace up.

Treatment, Split line; Swastika method:

fig. 78a; Spiral knot panel: 4 units:

fig. 78b Panel; 16 spiral knots, plain:

The panel is developed from the four unit
border, as above on page 268, fig. 76.

fig. 79 Same; with split ribbon openwork:

In figure 77, the path of the knot is split
by the "swastika" method; here, the
split ribbon work can only be produced
by the pencil-erase method, which
gives this lacy openwork effect.

fig. 80   Openwork Split Ribbon;
             pencil-erase method

Lightly pencil the
a   centre line.

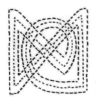

Slightly more heavily,
pencil either side of
b centre line.

Weave outlines only;
ink-lines are pencil-line
c thickness apart;

erase pencil when weaving
is completed; ink in with
d   brush.

— This is most effective
done very small scale.

fig. 81 Spiral knot – Two unit variation; from Tara Brooch pin head:

a

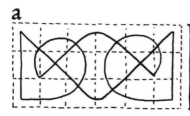

b

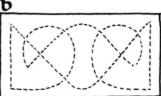

This arrangement, spirals back-to-back:

c

d

a. The knotline.
b. Pencil it in.
c. Outline and weave. This is broad band style.
d. Broad band may be given a fine inline which may be coloured in:

COLOUR THE CENTRE PORTION (SHADED)

fig. 82 Spiral Knot Panel; four units, back-to-back; from bone trial piece, Lagore Crannog.

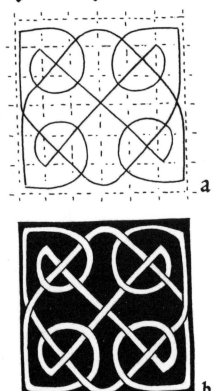

a

b

fig. 83 Dot-and-breakline Grid for Lagore Crannog knot:

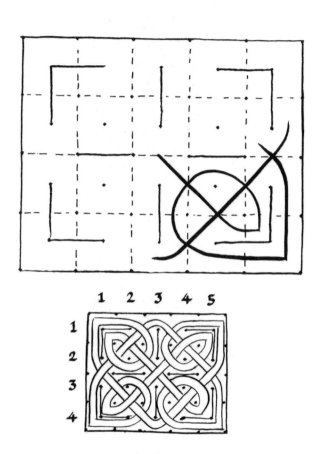

The primary grid is 5 spaces across, & 4 spaces down.

Fig. 84,a. Bird with Spiral Knot Neck,
from Book of Kells, folio 2 R:

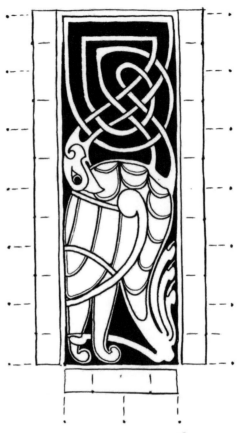

2 spaces across, 6 down,
on primary grid.

fig 84,b. Kells Bird with Spiral knot neck; canonical plan & variant:

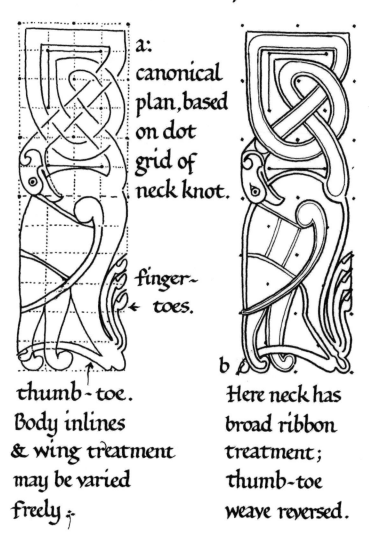

a: canonical plan, based on dot grid of neck knot.

finger-
← toes.

thumb-toe.
Body inlines
& wing treatment
may be varied
freely;

b

Here neck has
broad ribbon
treatment;
thumb-toe
weave reversed.

fig.85 Spiral Knot panel,
Ardagh Chalice layout:

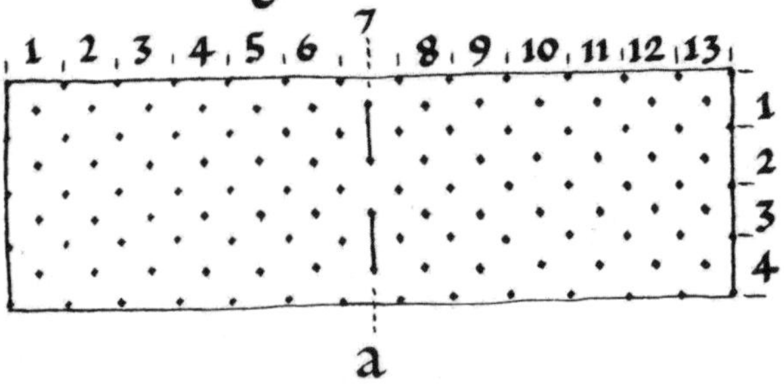

For this panel, lay out a square
grid of dots 13 across and 4 down;
lay the centre points of each of
the square cells, thus making
the secondary grid.

As this is an odd number of
spaces on the primary grid, the
vertical axis of symmetry falls
on the secondary grid, a, above.

Lay the first break lines on the axis;

fig. 86 Ardagh Chalice Panel; breaklines:

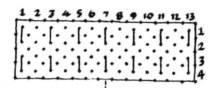

starting from the centre, repeat the pairs of secondary grid breaklines to each end, leaving two spaces between each pair:

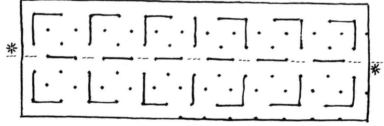

Next, arrange horizontal breaks thus: (note the horizontal axis* on primary) grid.

fig. 87 Ardagh Chalice Spiral Panel

The panel reflects the solar cycle

a

12 Apostles' names are inscribed below it

b

12 spirals; 2 groups of six; opposed
on either arm of cross horizontal or
vertical, "X" in centre; 4 groups of
three: solstice & equinoctial numbers.

fig.88   Ardagh Brooch; spiral knots;
row of three:

dots & breaks;   a   pencil..

breaks
&   b   ink..
dots;

pencil;   c   line..

pencil;   d   outline;

ink;   e   weave
&
fill in.

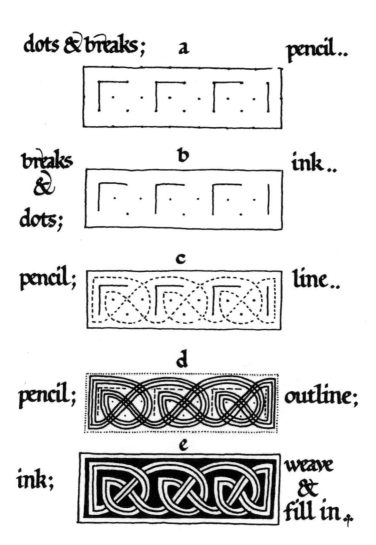

fig. 89

a,b,c : from Large Ardagh brooch.
d: from silver gilt
    brooch, Cavan.

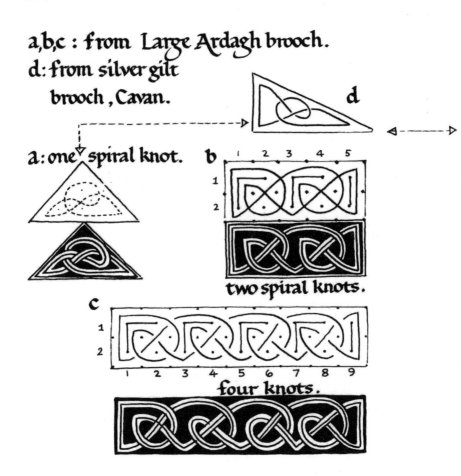

a: one spiral knot.   b

two spiral knots.

c

four knots.

Each repeat unit = 2 spaces wide.
Let n = number of repeat units;

fig. 90

a,b: Ardagh brooch.

compare this triangle, 89 d, with the example at 89a.

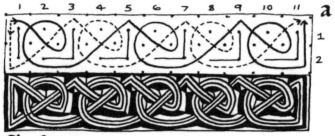

a

five knots.

b

six knots.

total number of spaces = 2 n + 1.

Thus, 4 knots = 9 ; 6 knots = 13.

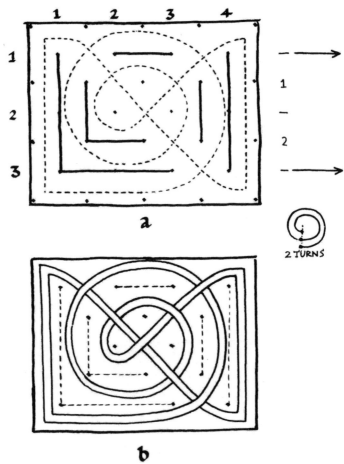

fig. 91 Spiral knot; two-turn spiral;
one unit; dot grid & breaklines:

a

1   2

2 TURNS

b

🙞 notice narrowness of path.∴

fig. 92 Compare one- and two-turn
spiral knot grids:
Compare figs 91 & 92:

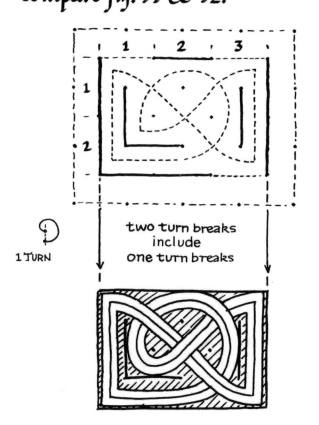

two turn breaks
include
one turn breaks

1 TURN

although same scale, fewer breaks &
less curvature allow path thickness:•

fig. 93 Two-Turn spiral knots, from
Lagore Crannog; row of 2 units:

The dots
were drilled
or pierced
in bone,
& the
break lines
incised to
form the
knot.

In all the spirals from lagore bone &
Ardagh brooch the proportions of path
width & flattened curve mean dot
grids were used.

fig. 94 Spiral Knots; Ardagh Brooch; two turns; row of three─:

a

b

KINK

c Plan for chip carving:

The flattening of the spirals as well as the corner kink indicate that the worker followed the canonical grid.

fig.95 Spiral panel ; 4 knots ;
2 turns ;

Here is the logical deduction which might have resulted from the bone~ carving class in the Crannog at Lagore.

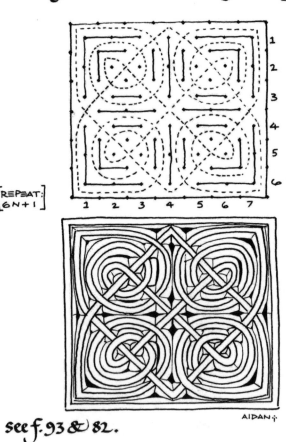

[REPEAT:
6N+1]

see f. 93 & 82.

AIDAN✝

fig.96 Ornamental Serif, Lindisfarne, folio.3

fig. 97 Spiral Knot; Lindisfarne; dot & grid construction:

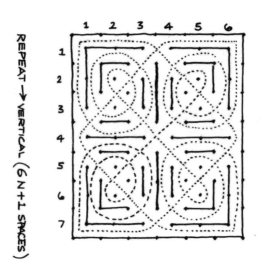

This is the construction of
the knot at *fig. 96*, which is
black path line on open, white
background. *Opposite*: more con~
ventional, white on black.

fig. 98 Lindisfarne spiral knot panel,
path/ground reversal,
white on black:

a

b

Any square panel may be made circular.

fig. 99 Spiral knot panel; 16 units; dot-&-break grid:

Let n equal number of repeat units:
Eleven spaces across; $2\frac{1}{2}n+1$, $n=4$.
Thirteen spaces down; $3n+1$, $n=4$.

fig.100 spiral knot panel; 16 Knots:

Background may be left open, or filled in.

fig. 101 Border Design, full page format; adapted from the Book of Durrow:

upper row: This form substitutes for crossover, thus as below

fig. 102 Durrow Border spiral knot;
single unit; dot grid, breakline &
keyline construction:

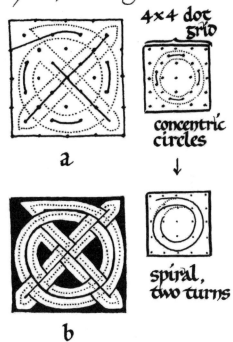

4×4 dot grid

concentric circles

a

↓

spiral, two turns

b

Where the ribbon is broad, parallel segments as here in the diagonals, or concentric segments as in the spiral, share a common edge, the keyline.

[295]

fig.103   Spiral Knots ; 2 units ; Construction :

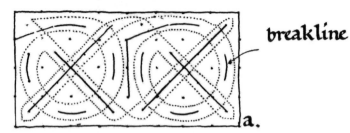

breakline

a.

a,b: dot grid & breaklines; diagonal keylines

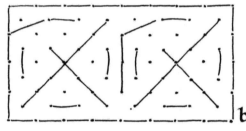

b.

c: Note that spiral keyline joins

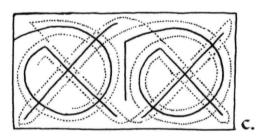

c.

together the breaklines.

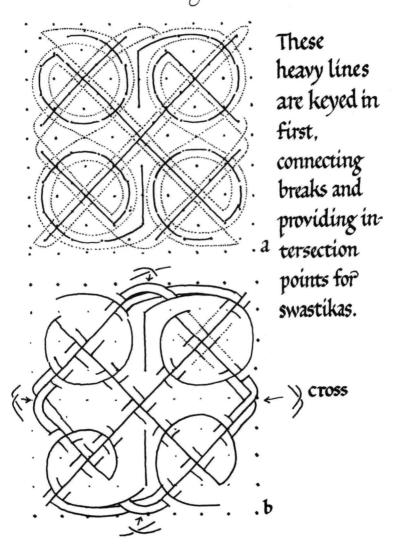

fig. 104 Spiral Knots; 4 units; Construction:

These heavy lines are keyed in first, connecting breaks and providing intersection points for swastikas.

a

←)) cross

b

fig. 105 Durrow Spiral knot panel; four units:

Look closely at this knot & compare it with the keyline-and-swastika method of previous page. The construction lines are still evident in the final stage, as here.

fig. 106 Durrow spiral knot panel; six units:

keyline   **a**   swastika

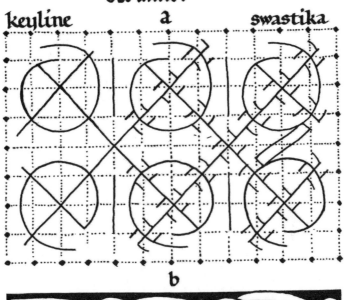

b

fig. 107 Durrow Spiral knot panel, with integrated frame ❖

chapter XI
Spiral
knot borders

fig. 108

Figure 109: Romilly Allen's twelve Elementary Knots

(Taken from "Proceedings of Society of Antiquarians of Scotland"
Romilly Allen, Celtic art lover & historian

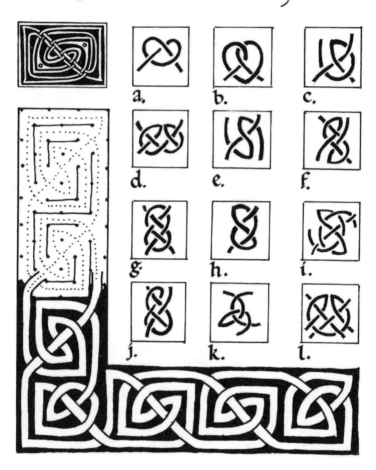

a.
b.
c.
d.
e.
f.
g.
h.
i.
j.
k.
l.

Figure 110: Analysis of Allen's knots.

Feb. 12, May 11, '83.
first published these in 1883.

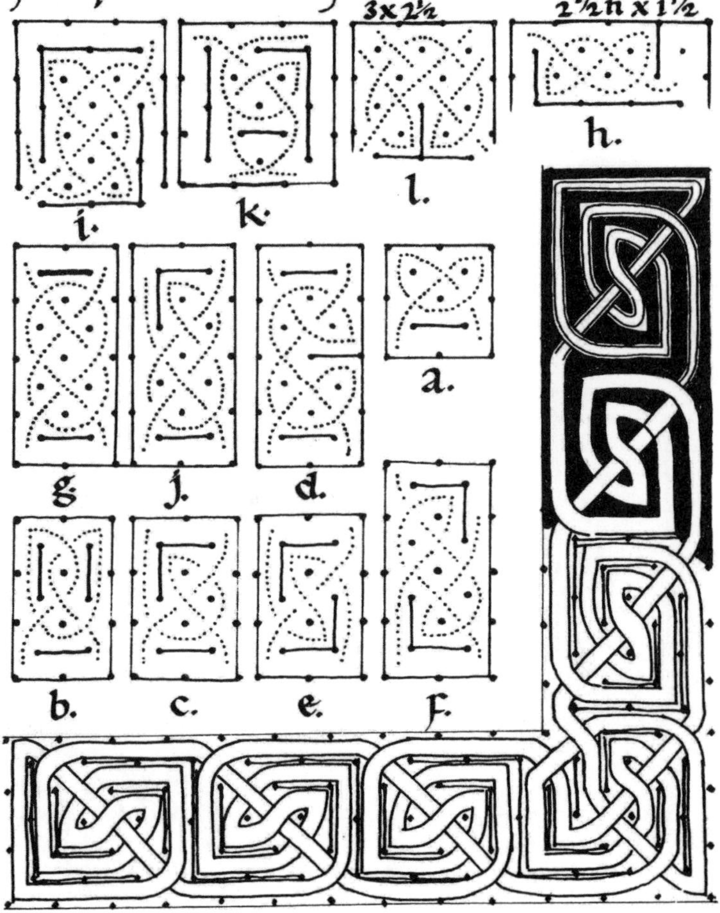

3 x 2½

2½ in x 1½

h.

i.

k.

l.

g.

j.

d.

a.

b.

c.

e.

f.

Figure 111: Spiral Border, Six Braid Knot.

The spiral border below right
has a different construction
for the mitred corner than here, left.
The change is æsthetically better.

Terminal

Mitre

The corner variants inspired
these square knots; also,
check out this split ribbon.

Figure 112 : Development of Spi...

Overleaf; fig. 113 : more spira...

Border from Eight-cord Braid

from Eight-Braid

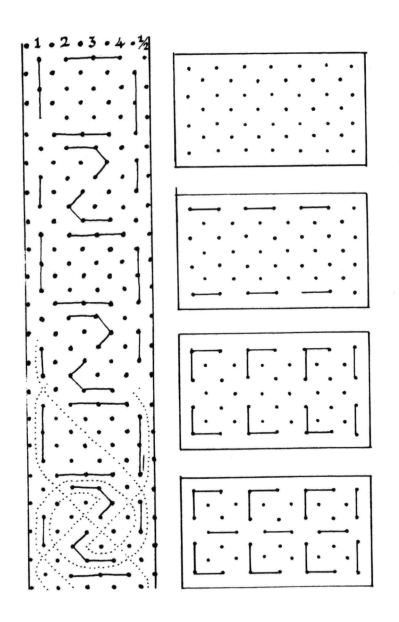

Fig. 113: Border-from South Cross, Clonmac-
noise, Ire.

[309]

Fig.114 four, five, eight & Ten cord knots.
eight cord border from Book of Durrow.

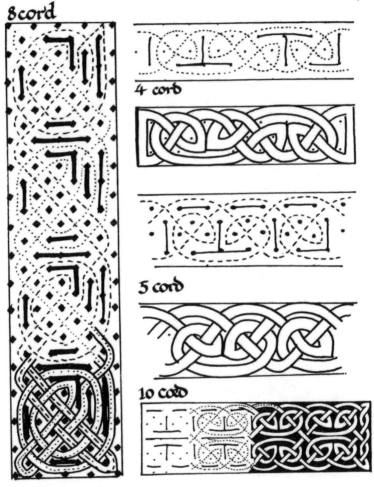

8 cord

4 cord

5 cord

10 cord

Appendix : Triangular Knots

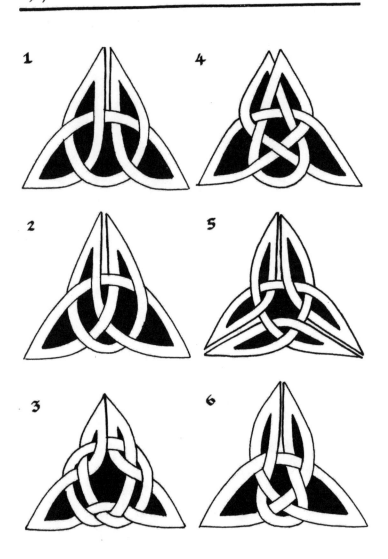

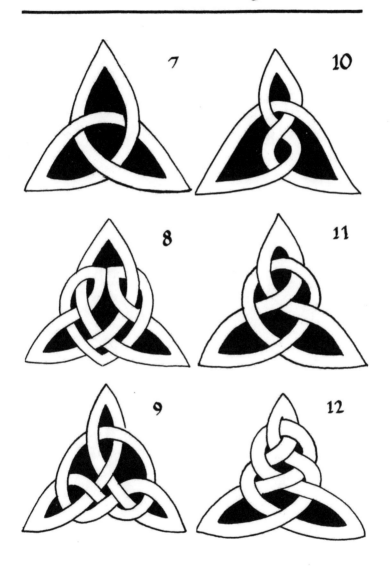

appendix

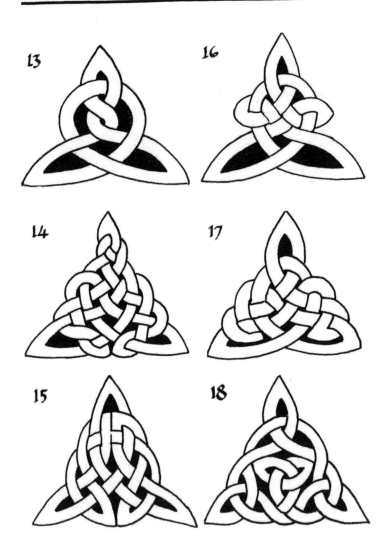

13

16

14

17

15

18

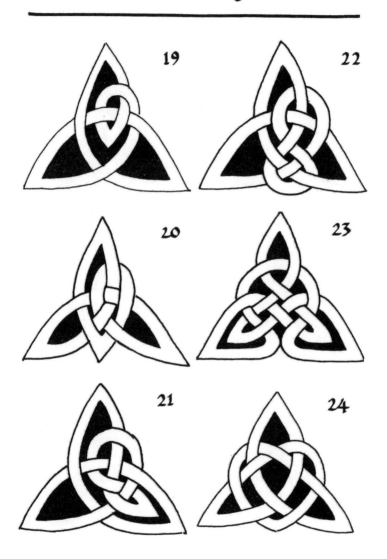

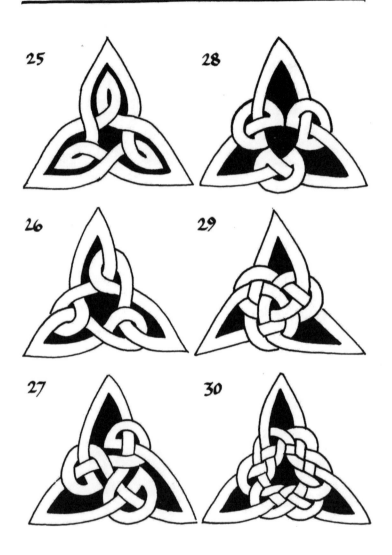

25   28

26   29

27   30

31
34
32
35
33
36

Appendix

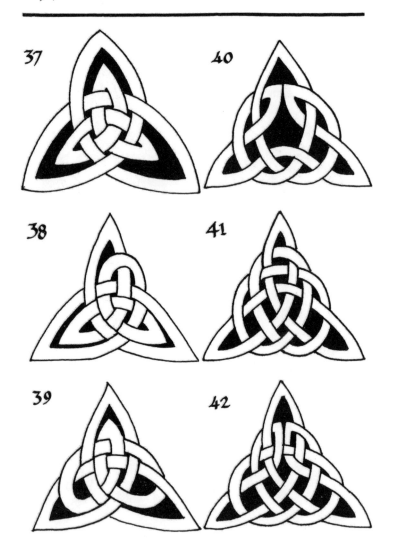

37

40

38

41

39

42

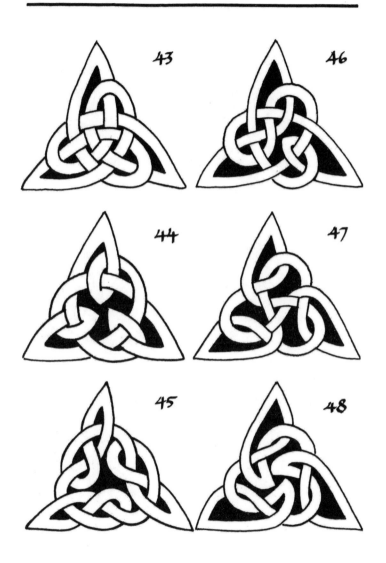

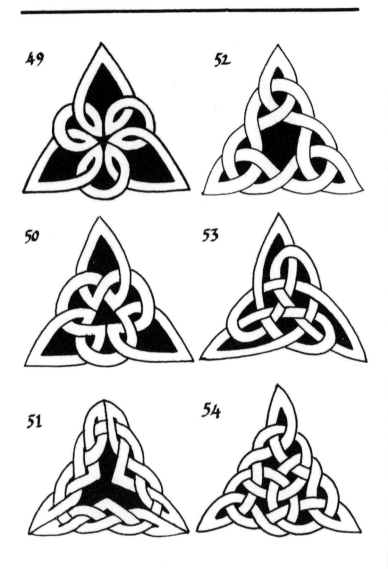

49

52

50

53

51

54

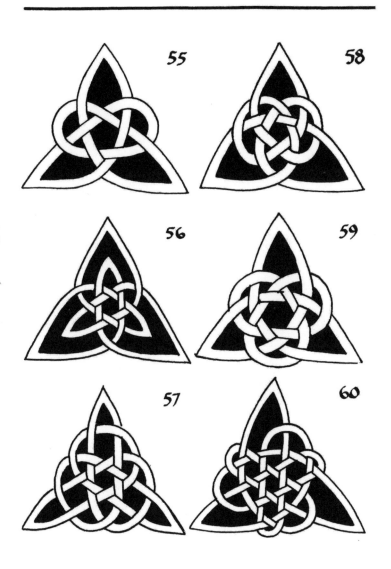

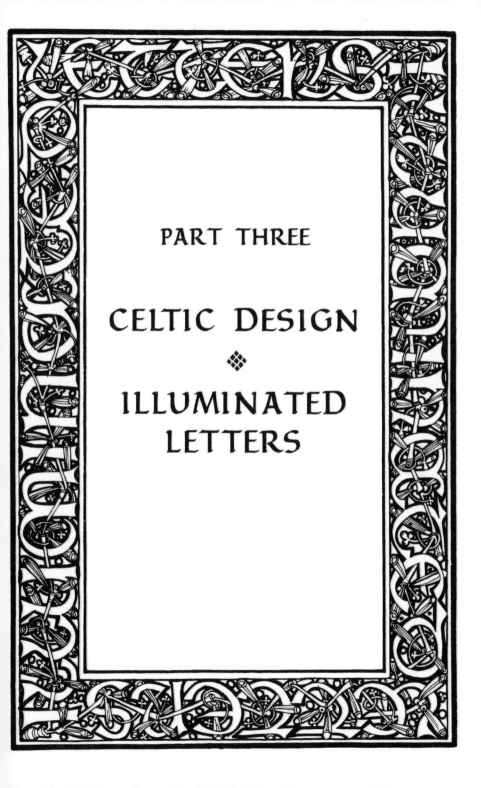

PART THREE

CELTIC DESIGN

❖

ILLUMINATED
LETTERS

✻

BOOKS ABOUT CELTIC illumination usually present us with colour reproductions that focus on the most elaborate examples as tightly packed with details as a Persian carpet. This book is a collection of simpler ornamental letters picked out and rendered as line drawings, ready to be coloured. As such it is a resource for Celtic artists, calligraphers and crafts people, and indeed anybody that shares an interest in the inventiveness of the Celtic

scribes. In their own day, there must
have been reference manuals, similar to
studio text books, passed down from
one generation to the next. I hope
this series will serve in the same way
for a new generation.

CELTIC ILLUMINATION, THE EARLY DEVELOPMENT

A VERY EARLY PSALM BOOK, the Cathach of St Columba, c. 600, is decorated with letters in Irish script treated with spirals of a pure Celtic style. Some have small animal heads, fish perhaps, and crosses of a type found in sixth-century Ireland. It is the earliest surviving evidence of the first developments of Celtic illumination. The letters are built up with broad and narrow penstrokes in a dark brown ink, with red dots outlining the shape and yellow voids inside the letters.

[329]

Chapter 1

Fig.1 Letter M from the Cathach.

Even in black and white as in this M, the dots add a half-tone which heightens the white voids between the penstrokes of the curves, and between the spirals and the styl-ized birdhead terminals. The split curves form moons; the terminals are an ancient Celtic art motif, called divergent trum-pet pattern.

Fig.2 Letter Q, the Cathach.

In this built-up black letter, the split of
the curves has been reduced to a sliver of a
moon, toned down even further by hatch-
ing. From the spiral foot leaps a long-
jawed, fish-like creature, a dolphin
perhaps, bearing a cross. Two curves on
its neck might be read as gills. Its
laughing mouth is a black sub-triangle
relieved by a white lens, another detail
of Celtic spiral treatment.

[331]

Fig. 3 Natural uncials, Luxeuil c. 600.

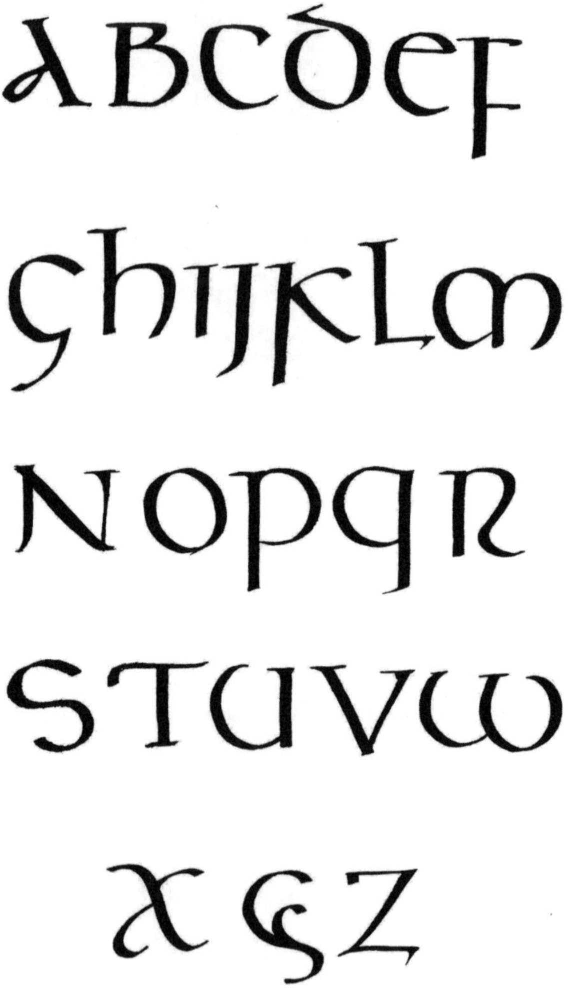

A B C D E F

G h i j k l m

N O P Q R

S T U V W

X G Z

[332]

Fig.4 Irish half-uncials, Bobbio c.600.

abcdef

ghijkl

mnopq

nſtuv

wxℊ⁊

[333]

FIG.5 Monogram DS, the Cathach.

I nnomine

⨰ & : in uirtate

ōs exaudionacionem

T HIS UNCIAL D has a fish tail with a
pelta, diverging to a trumpet opposite a plain divergence that counters curve
with corner, ending in a discreet spiral. Inside, a red dot-and-slash filler, a main –
stay of Celtic ornament for centuries.

[334]

R ED dotting is the first stage of illumi-
nating Celtic letters. Rubrication, as
this is called, adds a dimension of colour to
that of contrast. The effect is that of a tint:
by breaking up the red with white inter-
spaces, the eye mixes the solid colour with
the gaps to perceive pink. Dotting makes
the letter appear to float up off the page and
glow rosily. The letters D and S of *fig.* 5
may be dotted using *fig.* 1 as a guide.
Trace around the letters with a light
pencil line first, then dot along the line,
and erase it. Use a fine-tip red marker.
A NOTHER FEATURE of Celtic illumination is called the *diminuendo*,
where the large capital is led into harmony
with the text by an intermediate letter or

FIG.6 NOLI , the Cathach.

letters, smaller than the initial, but larger than the text. The Cathach is a very early example of this, fig.6. The space between the uprights of the N features a long-stemmed cross combining both the Greek and the Roman form. Below the cross the bar of the letter undulates, and suggests the form of a fish. But as well as the obvious symbols, there is a geometric, numerical symbol in

the way the diminuendo forms a 3: 4 triangle. These two numbers are significant as
relating to the Trinity and the cross, but also
as they sum up to seven, the symbolic theme
of the Book of Revelation of St John, who
saw seven golden candlesticks, and in their
midst a lamb with seven horns and seven
eyes, who said

> I am the Alpha and the Omega,
> the beginning and the end,
> the first and the last.

LPHA AND OMEGA turn up in another early Gospelbook, the Codex Usserianus, named after the seventeenth century Dubliner, Bishop Ussher. It provides a clue to the type of full-page design that may once have served as a frontispiece for Celtic manuscripts at the end of the sixth century. The Ussher Codex contains such a page in the form of the monogram XP, or Chi-Rho, outlined in dots, fig. 7. The Greek letter X is rotated into a cross with a shaft twice as long as the transverse, and divided by it so that it suggests the three-in-one with equal units above and below the middle bar. The page has been ruled with lines scored beforehand as for a page of text; the centre square is 12 ruled spaces deep.

Fig. 7 Cross - monogram page, Ussher Codex,
c. 600.

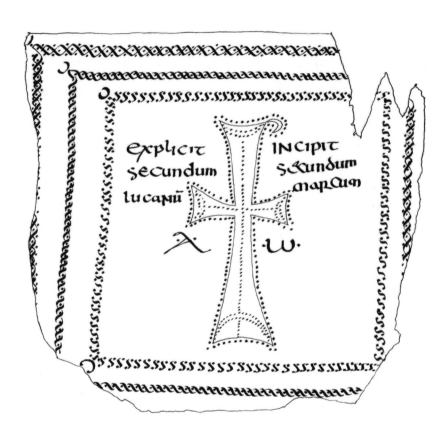

explicit
secundum
lucam

incipit
secundum
marcum

A. .w.

Fig.8   Pattern of the Usshen monogram.

In the upper left is the Latin word Explicit, which means, here ends (Luke). This is balanced diagonally opposite, at bottom right, by the Greek letter W, Omega, which means the end (or last letter of the alphabet).

In the upper right, Incipit – here begins (Mark), is mirrored lower left by Alpha, the beginning (of the alphabet), recalling the words of the Book of Revelation, I am the Alpha and the Omega, the beginning and the end.

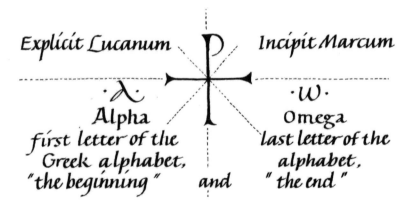

Explicit Lucanum   Incipit Marcum

·λ·   ·W·
Alpha   Omega
first letter of the   last letter of the
Greek alphabet,   alphabet,
"the beginning"   and   "the end"

THE DIVISION OF THE CROSS SHAFT
by the arm in the ratio 1:2 refers to
the creation of the two, heaven and
earth, by the one, God. The horizontal
arm moves between the two parts as
in Genesis 1:2, where "the Spirit of
God moved upon the waters". Then
follow the seven days of Creation, each
a pair of opposites: Day and Night;
waters above and below the firma —
ment; Earth and Seas; sun and moon;
birds and animals; Adam and Eve.
God rested on the seventh day, symbolized as the still centre of a circle divided by its radius. Thus not only the
number seven but also the hexagonal
marigold motif of *fig.* 10 are symbols
of the birth of the cosmos.

[341]

THE USSHER MONOGRAM PAGE
is an intentional play of number
symbols; for example, the 1:2 proportion
of the cross width to height, as we have
seen. This is also the ratio of the two
strokes of letter chi, or *X*, where the
thin is twice as long as the thick one.
In the monogram the diagonal cross,
chi, is rotated to become the upright
cross. However, the pattern of the diagonals is emphasized in the pattern of the
inscription *fig. 8*. But the upright
cross introduces its own symbolism,
foursquare, and quarter. The pattern
of the text is divided left and right,
Luke and Mark; and also above and below, Latin overhead, Greek beneath.

APART FROM THIS BILINGUAL PLAY
there is the reference to the Revelation of St John, Alpha and Omega,
which is associated with the number
seven that links the first book of the
Old Testament with the last book of the
New Testament. The cross in the centre
of the square is naturally fourfold, but
its proportions of 2:1 make it tripartite. The pattern of the text supports
this three- and fourfoldness, for there
are four lines of writing divided into
three in the upper quadrant and one in
the lower, a trinity symbol, 3:1. As
well, the text is divided symmetrical-
ly into two pillars flanking the vertical axis of the cross shaft, and with
it make three columns altogether.

[343]

FIS.9   Dot-and-stroke pattern, Ussher.

Start with a single row of dots, then add the stroke. Think of the spot as the centre of a circle, and the stroke follows the curve over the one and under the next.

Start with two rows of dots. This pattern depends on a sharp contrast between thick and thin, a basic broad nib exercise.

Start with two rows, then add the third as the centre of each square cell. Or think of it as a five-spot if you prefer. Do one zig-zag, then put in the second.

THREE AND FOUR RECUR IN THE BOR-
DER, *fig.* 9, where we see the middle
border is a pattern based on a single row
of dots and horizontal s-scroll pen strokes;
the inside border based on two dots and a
vertical s-scroll; the outer border based on
three rows, a synthesis of saltire and diamond forming a two-strand helix. So we
have a trinity of square borders, the outer-
most a repeat of the saltire and dots, X as
used in *fig.* 5, *line* 2, a Cathach contraction
for Christ. The corners of the squares are
decorated with horns, twelve in all; there
are twelve sides in all, as in the edges of a
cube; the ground plan of the centre area
is twelve square. Twelve and seven, 3 x 4
and 3+4, numbers of the New Jerusalem
and Genesis are the themes used here.

Fig.10   Carpet page, Chronicle of Orosius,
           showing Geometry.

Fig. 11   Page opposite carpet page, Orosius

Praeceptus tuis pa-

rui beatissime pater agustine ab
q: utinam tam efficaciter quam ly
benter quamquam ego in utra vis
partem parum explicito movear
Recte nean secur egerim t ad
iudicio laborasti utrumnehoc qua ua
peter possim egoautem solius oboedientiae
sic tamen cum uoluntate conatuq: deboray
timonio contencui sum. Nam cum magna in
gmpatris familias domo cum sint malta diuer
si generis animalia adiumento familiarii rei
comoda noneft tamen contum cura porere
ma quib: solis natura insamere uoluntate
: alid quod prae:- arantur urgerem experin

T HE NEXT MAJOR DEVELOPMENT was the full-page ornament facing a page-length initial followed by a banner headline extending to the right-hand margin. This combination became the trademark of seventh-century Celtic manuscripts, but we find a prototype in the copy of the Chronicle of Orosius, from the Columban foundation of Bobbio, written about 620 in an early script like that of the Ussher Codex. The full-page pattern is based on a 10 x 12 square grid, as shown in *fig. 10*. The 3 x 4 theme which we found in the Ussher Codex turns up here in the construction of the circles, as in *fig. 12*. The four corner circles each have 3 rings; the centre circle has 8 rings, with seven interstitial bands.

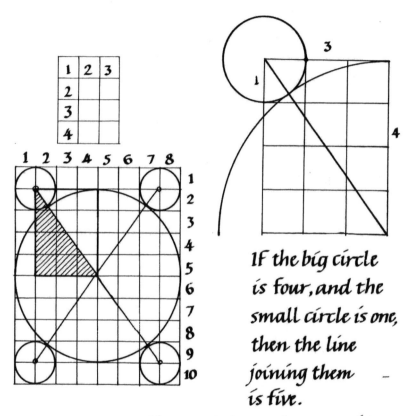

If the big circle
is four, and the
small circle is one,
then the line
joining them
is five.

However this diagonal is the longest side
of the right-angle triangle shown shaded,
which therefore has sides 3 x 4 x 5.

Fig.13   Merovingian letter N,
         Commentary of St. Jerome.

Fig. 14 Initial page from Durham Fragment II.

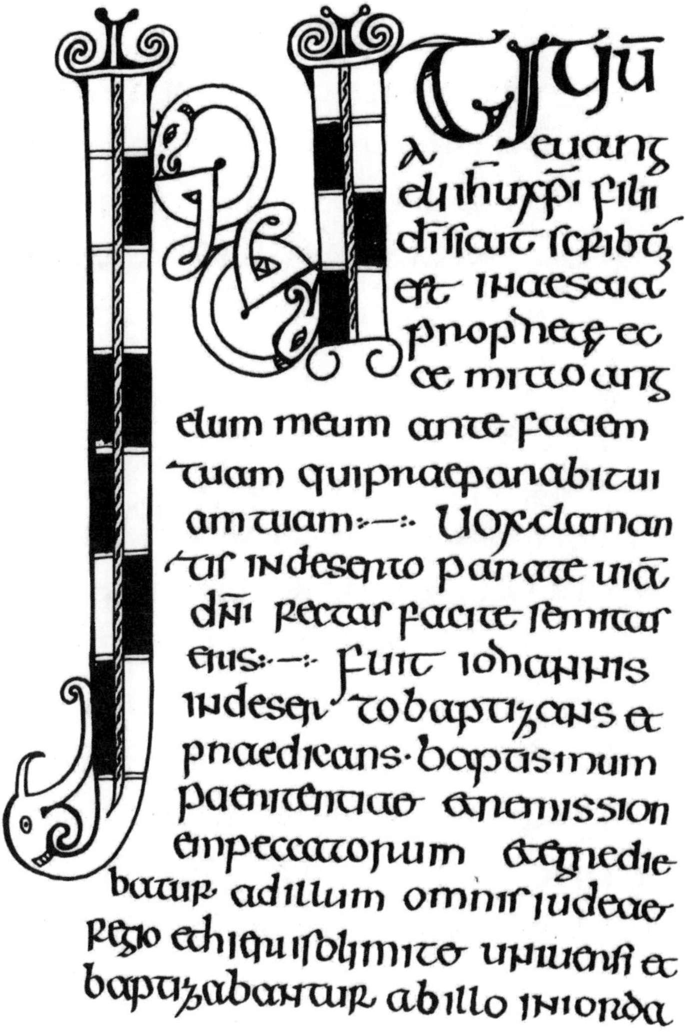

THE OPENING UP OF THE LETTERFORM
introduces fresh scope for ornament,
in the body of the letter itself. We now have
a new order of initial. In the Chronicle of
Orosius, a two-cord braid fills the descender. Although it is applied as an after-
thought, by the rubricator, the idea of
decorating the letter with a two-cord
braid quickly spread from scribe to scribe,
and soon made its appearance as an integ-
ral part of the pen-drawn letter, as we
can see from a fragment of a Gospel book
that apparently came to the cathedral
library of Durham from elsewhere,
fig. 14, but cannot be much later than its
prototype from Bobbio of c.620, fig. 13. In
this example from a Commentary of St. Jer-
ome, we find the short ascender has been

divided into four boxes, separated by three
lines. In the Durham fragment, *fig* 14, the
ascender is divided into four parts separated by two lines. Both have spiral serifs.
Both have animal cross-bars, the pair
from Durham have gills, clearly referring
to fish. The fish in the Bobbio example
leap out of a *chí*-cross centrepiece, based
on the form of the letter, χ, the curves
drawn out as spirals. The eels of Durham are centred on the cursive, minuscule
letter, x, the multiplication sign. The
style of the two letters is different, that
of Bobbio is Merovingian, and the
one from Durham is Celtic. But the
similarities are so striking, they must
have a common model.

Chapter 1

WHAT WE SEE IN THE DURHAM fragment from the first quarter of the seventh century is the beginning of the synthesis of ornamental forms from many different sources encountered, collected and copied by the scribes on their travels abroad. Now a shift of emphasis took place, away from the monastery as a communal sanctuary of ascetics towards a training ground for evangelism. Whereas before, the art of illumination had hidden itself from the eyes of the world, now it increasingly had to be attractive ; no longer the monopoly of the scribes, for artisans were beginning to elaborate on the basic elements, the new art was about to spring into the light of day .

MAJOR INITIALS from the GOLDEN AGE of CELTIC ART

HE BOOK OF DURROW represents the first flowering of the tradition in the early seventh century when the ornament was mainly spiral and knotwork, *figs 15, 16*. Here we see the letters outlined and filled with knot borders, while the serifs and voids are filled with Celtic spirals derived from ancient metalwork patterns: divergent trumpets and occasional horse~head terminals.

[355]

FIS.15 Letters F and Q, from the Book of Durrow.

THE amazing thing about the Book of Durrow is its scale, only 9¼ x 6½ in (24 x 16.5 cm), not much larger than this book. The letters of fig. 15 are reproduced to about the same size, drawn with a fine nib and hairline brush in the original, though I have used technical pens here. The letters were drawn in a brownish black, like the patina in the sunken back - grounds of gold brooches, and col - oured with a bright, cold lemon - yellow tempera, imitating gold inlaid with enamel, with warm plum-red and deep copper-green. To people unaccustomed to painting it must have looked magically real - istic, akin to photo-realism today.

Fig.16 Monogram IN, from the Book of Durrow.

Fig.17 Monogram INP, from Corpus Christi ms. 197.

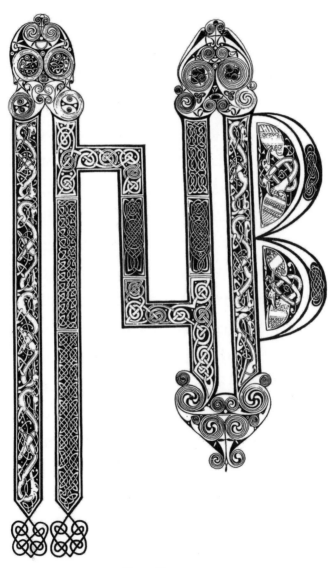

FROM THE SEVENTH to the ninth century, artists and scribes travelled continually from one Celtic monastery to another, giving and exchanging books which were copied and recopied. The models were transmitted rapidly far and wide, new developments catching on alongside older forms, transitional designs appearing beside fixed conventions. Some decorators used designs learnt at school from older masters passing on motifs familiar to them from their own early days. Accordingly it is no surprise to see Durrow-style animals alongside birds of a generation later in the Corpus Christi College Library, ms.197, *fig.17*.

The knot at the bottom of the N in Corpus Christi turns up in the Book of Lindisfarne fifty years later, at the top of the same letter, as in *figs.*17, 26. In Lindisfarne the knot is decked with dogheads whose ears connect in spirals, a trick inherited by MacRegol in his INP, *fig.* 18, a century later. An even greater span lies between the INP of Corpus Christi and that of MacRegol, so similar in design as to suggest a common model, *figs* 17, 18. MacRegol also preserves features of Durham II in the dog's tongue, *figs* 18, 20; also, compare the knot of *figs* 19, 20.

[361]

Fig. 18 Monogram INP, from the Book
of MacRegol.

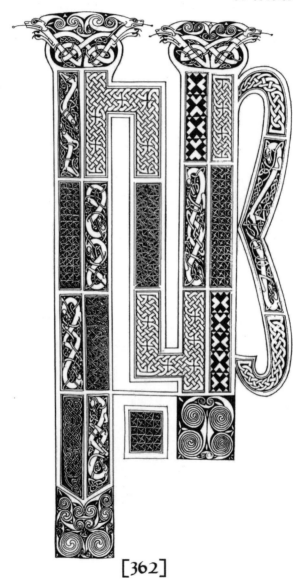

[362]

Another example of the diffusion of motifs, over time as well as distance, is the instance of the white curl at the nape of the neck of the dog and the bird heads of Durham II. This turns up in the Book of Kells, fig.47, in the late eighth century. A similar pattern of conservation and exchange of decorations occurring between many schools is found on the Continent, among those established by Irish monks of the sixth century. But with the Anglo-Irish foundation of Echternach, Celtic manuscripts were circulated throughout the seventh century such as we find at Cologne Cathedral and Trèves, St Gall and St Willibrord, figs 21-24.

FIG. 19 Monogram LIB, the Book of MacRegol.

[364]

Fig.20 Letters A, M, from Durham Fragment II.

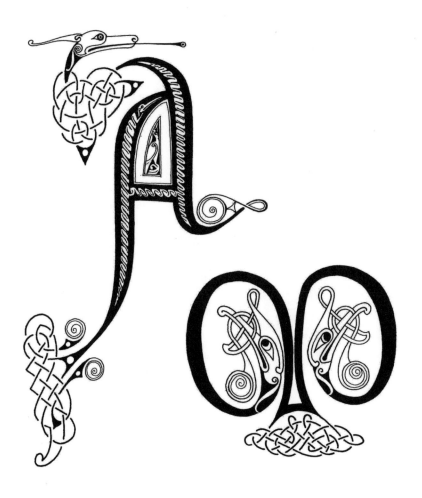

FIG. 21   letters D, D, from Cologne Cathedral ms. 213.

The manuscript from Cologne, fig. 21 has a fish tailed D like that of the Cathach, fig. 5, converted to black line knots as in Durham, fig. 20, and filled with spirals like that of fig. 27.

Fig.22   Letter N, from the Book of Trèves.

The Trèves N has no animals but for
this exception, with birdhead quad-
rupeds. The style is that of the time
of Durrow, but was written a century later at a monastery near Echternach.

[367]

Chapter 11

FIG. 23   Letter Q. from the Book of St Gall.

[368]

FIG. 24 Letter Q from the Book of St Willibrord.

THE ANIMAL STYLE of the Book of Trèves is not unique. The Cologne manuscript also has a hybrid form, the long-beaked birdhead attached to quadruped hind legs, fig. 21. This style persists well into the eighth century on the Continent, a parallel development reflecting an influence other than Irish or Northumbrian : Pictish, for in~ stance. Or it may represent a survival stemming from an early, cherished model ; or the result of a strong conser- vative tradition. Lacking animal patterns, the Book of Willibrord -also known as the Book of Echternach- did little to alter the influence of the early transitional style on the Continent , fig. 24.

FIG.25   MA and D, the Book of Lindisfarne.

FIG. 26   Letter N, from Lindisfarne.

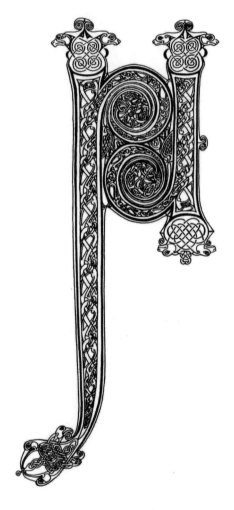

Here the spiral patterns are pure Celtic, very similar to those of Durrow.
Also, compare the M of *fig.* 25 with
that of *fig.* 20. The N of Lindisfarne,
fig. 26 , is filled with birds, a late seventh-century development.

[373]

FIG. 28   Letter M, from the Vatican
Barbarini ms. 570.

The tradition began to lapse in Eng –
land after the Book of Lindisfarne, as
seen by the Book of Cerne, fig. 29, and
the Book of Uigbald, abbot of Lindisfarne about 800, fig. 28.

FIG. 29   Letter A, from the Book of Cerne.

[375]

FIG. 30   Letter Q, from the Maihingen Gospels.

FIG. 31   Letter X, from the Maihingen Gospels.

ON THE CONTINENT, however, the Irish-Northumbrian fusion epitomised by the Book of Lindisfarne continued unabated in the eighth century as we have seen from the Book of Trèves. In the Maihingen Gospels, figs 30, 31 we see a fine example of creative, original work which integrates and ramifies the innovations of the previous centuries, and so furthers the tradition. But the best example of this vitality and creativity, which are so necessary to a living, growing tradition is of course the Book of Kells, to which we now turn in order to understand the elements of Celtic design as applied to decorated letters.

DECORATED ALPHABET

HIS ALPHABET IS DRAWN from the Book of Kells (see reading list page 480) . In the original each letter is finely dotted all around with red, closely following the outside of the letter about a millimetre from it, where the dots are of the same dimension, and the same distance apart. Enclosed areas are not dotted. The letters may be drawn with a wide-nibbed calligraphy pen, requiring manipulation, or drawn with a pencil and inked-in with a fine brush, such as a size zero sable. The ink to use is chinese black, softened with the addition of a drop or so of vermilion and lemon yellow water colour. Paper should be a good quality , and extra-smooth , not very absorbent.

Opposite :

a

Tripartite division of enclosure provides a suggestion for void treatment of other letters, such as P or Q .

b

Central division a triangular pennant pan-elled with step pattern .

c

Pennant bracketed by birds; lionhead ter-minal biting lion cub.

d

Pennant emblazoned with a variant of the triquetra .

Fig. 32

a   b

c   d

Fig. 33

The body spirals in a diamond forming a path of the open ground converging on a chevron arrowhead.

a   b

a

The C is continuous with the uncial A ,
with lionhead and triquetra knot .

b

Two sub-semicircles filled with knotwork
frame an angular O containing an asterisk.

[383]

Fig. 35

Triangular flag-serif is decorated with
a spiral mask, with triskele eyes and a
marigold motif for a mouth. Inside, a
roundel of two lions.

Opposite: a
Here is a spiral space filler that could be adapted to letters b, c, p, q.

Fig.36

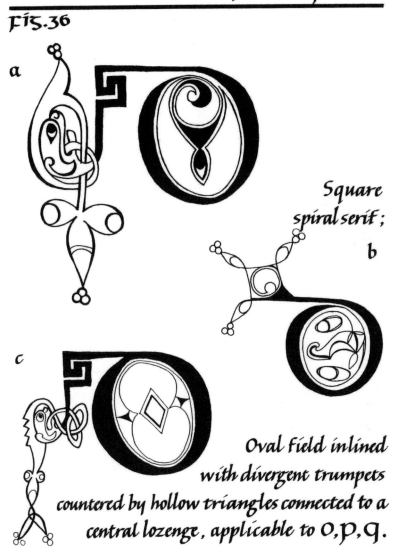

a

Square
spiral serif;

b

c

Oval field inlined
with divergent trumpets
countered by hollow triangles connected to a
central lozenge, applicable to o, p, q.

Fig. 37   Monograms EGO, ER, ERA, E.

a

b

c

d

Previous page:

a

Triquetral dog pattern adapted from a roundel.

b

Lionhead terminal with carpet-beater knot.

c

The larger knot here is useful in a long triangular area like this.

d

Upper section inline relieved by divergent trumpets, useful treatment for filling a tight area, as in R. Lower, triquetra knot adapted to a semicircle.

OF ALL THE SURVIVING CELTIC
MANUSCRIPTS, our single most
valuable source of letter forms is the
Book of Kells, because it is so continuously decorated throughout. It is extraor-
dinary that between the two types of
letters collected here - the decorated black
letter and the animal alphabet which
were used interchangeably, we have almost the whole Latin alphabet; apart
from letters J and W, unknown to the
scribes, K and Y were rare. Not sur-
prisingly, no paragraphs in the Book of
Kells begin with X or Z. Otherwise, we
lack only letters F in this and G, M in
the animal alphabet.

This half-uncial G has a crossbar suitable
for that of the letter T.

Overleaf:

a

An integration of serif and ponytail that would
also work for uncial M.

b

Fine knot treatment for ascender serif, and a
bearded head that might apply to a C.

[389]

Fig. 39

a

b

c

d

1H.

FIS. 40

Split curve and back-
ward ascender are
both archaic features.
Compare fig. 39, a,b.

Previous page:

c

Spiral lion
lacks forelegs. The supporting bird does not be-
long to the letter, but adds a decorative touch.

d

Lion's-paw motif at the foot serif. The gap at
the base is bridged by the drunkard's-path
motif, as if the inline suffers a fear of open spaces.

FÍꞬ.41 MonoꞬram ILL.

*A chicken contemplates a swash knot ending
in a trefoil or a bunch of berries. The serifs have
the lion's-paw motif.
Two L's , one with a drunkard's-path inline
and one without.*

[392]

Fig.42 Three letters based on previous figure.

E ACH OF THE DECORATED LETTERS
is unique, a variation on a theme,
inviting further changes. Elements of
one letter may be swapped for another.
Serifs may be interchanged, mutated.
You can take one ascender, one descender, one terminal, one ovoid and apply
them to the letters of figs 3, 4, to make
your own alphabet. Or make up your
own letters.

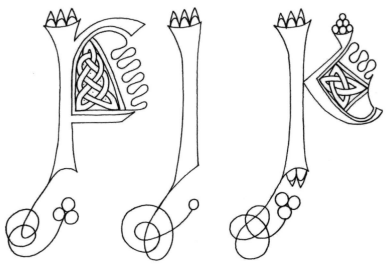

Fig.43

This human head terminal could be adapted to a C or a K. The knot could also be used in an h or n.

Opposite: a

Knot work serifs with lion head descender. The serifs of the A are subtle, a synthesis of knot and spiral.

b

A fully decorated uncial N, with knotwork and single spirals, drunkard's-path, wheel-in-circle and step pattern brackets.

[394]

Fíg.44

a   b

Monogram NA.

Perfectly symmetrical bird pattern roundel,
adapted to internal ovoid.

Lion's tongue ends in a lentoid knot. Interior
is filled with a pure Celtic spiral treatment.

Fig.46

The oval is filled with a beautiful spiral pattern, based on a regular circular design. The upper serif is a sitting duck. The lionhead serif has a curling lock of white-on-black typical of the Durham Fragment II, as in fig. 20 above.

[397]

Fig. 47

Typical three-part division of the ovoid.
Spiral knot in serif with shamrocks.

Opposite :

a   Here triangle and trefoil combine.

b   This letter is pointed on the left-hand side .

c   Ovoid pattern of zigzag and arches .

Fig.48

a

b

c

Fig.49

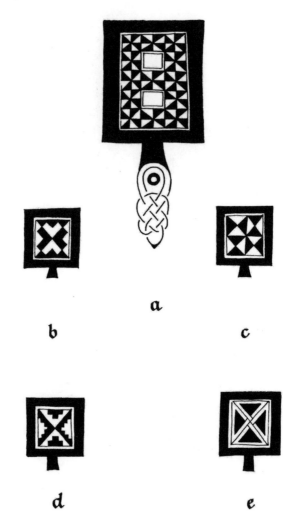

a

b

c

d

e

FIS. 50   Monogram OR .

This left-hand corner is decorated with a knot
based on lozenge
and saltire,

called the
FORMA
FORMARUM ,   or 'form of forms'.

Previous page:

Angular Q with fylfot-tile diaper and a
carpet-beater knot on the descender.
Also, four tile variations.

FIG. 51

Matching pair
with simple spirals.

a

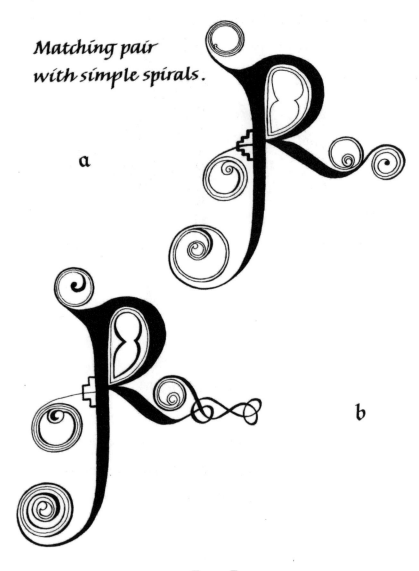

b

Fig.52

Hollow dart motif on head serif.

a

*Lionhead foot
continues
up to spiral.*

b

Fig. 53   Monogram SV   Monogram SCI

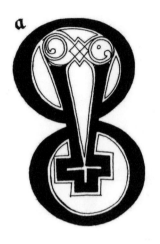

a

Pure abstract form, the waist of the S is hidden by the superimposed V to make it appear like two circles in a figure eight.

b

Monogram plainly outlined.

FIG. 54   Monogram TUN. Monogram TU.

a

This animal head has two long ears, eye presented frontally rather than in profile, and no line dividing the cheek from the jaw. This is how the hare is conventionally rendered.

b

Lion bites his own forelock.

Integrated spirals
and knot
link the serifs.
The treatment
of the spirals
is unique.

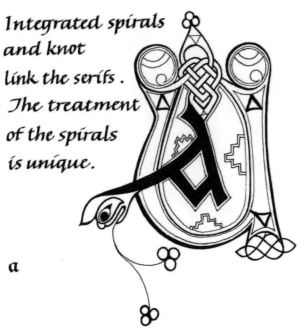

a

The bird filler
would be good
in the upper part
of e.

b

a This lion head sports a knot which metamorphoses into a spiral and a tree-of-life growing from a horn-of-plenty.

Fig. 57

Another spiral-knot serif, this one very subtly integrates with the inline of the letter.

DECORATED AMPERSANDS

HE AMPERSAND is a com—pound of two letters, Et, the latin word Et, meaning and; in the ampersand the crossbar of the E continues into the body of the T, leaving the bar of the T hanging there. The ampersand of today is a favourite of letter artists for the wide variety of its forms : & ; ℰ ; ¢ ; ℰ̣ ; & ; ℰ ; ℭ. The Celtic scribes obviously loved it too, and nowhere is it presented with so much of the shape-shifter's art as in the Book of Kells, from which these examples have been drawn.

Fig.58

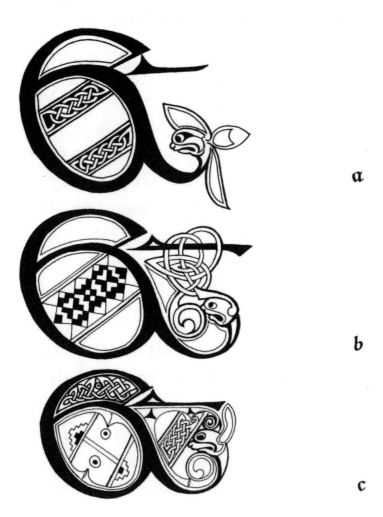

a

b

c

a

b

c

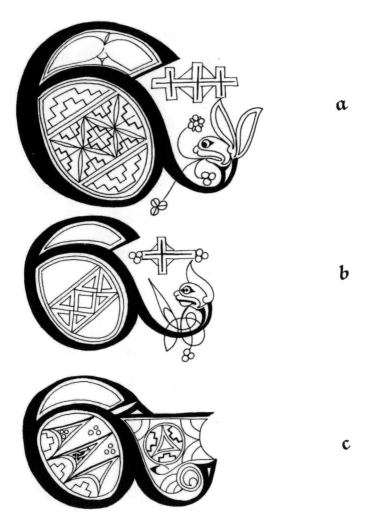

a

b

c

a

b

Fíg. 62

a

b

Fig.63

a

b

Fig. 64

a

b

Fig.65

a

b

FIG. 66

a

b

AMPERSANDS PROVIDE A GREAT BODY OF VARIATIONS on a single letter form, in this case the mono-gram ET. As we have seen above, page 393, a whole alphabet may be derived from just one or two decorated letters. This applies also to the ampersands on these pages. Each ampersand has a cross-bar with a serif and a terminal, except in a few cases where the bar is converted to a pure ornament, as *fig. 59 a*. The regular cross-bar treatments may be applied to the letter T or the half-uncial Ʒ. Likewise, the terminal of the T part of the ampersand may be applied not only to T, but also to the other half-uncials that have corresponding terminals, such as

A, C, E, K, L, R, X, Z. Thus a lionhead terminal could be generalized throughout these letters, with variations from the wide range to choose in both this and in the previous chapter. Or we might instead choose a human-head terminal, fig. 62, or a rabbit-head terminal, fig. 63 a. In either case we should have a very different alphabet as a result. The E part of the ampersand contains a narrow void or half-lunette, which may be applied to E, or the loop of an R. The larger void may be applied to the half-uncials A, B, D, O, P, Q; the treatment of the open space between cross-bar and terminal may be applied to the letters C, K, T, X.

ANIMAL ALPHABET

HIS ALPHABET also comes from the Book of Kells, and may be used interchangeably with that of chapter III, as minor initials with a text of Irish half-uncials. These initials may be coloured with black ink backgrounds and a halo effect of red dots. Or you may want to paint the letter with tempera colours, as for example on the cover of this book. I drew these with technical pens, using a medium nib throughout, with fine nib inline and thick for outline.

[421]

a   b

Two lions
with their
front legs crossed.

Single lion,
with
studded treatment.

Fig.68

In the previous figure there are two approaches to animal lettering. In fig. 67 a, the letter is made up of two lions. In the accompanying letter, the letter is the main part, with a lion's head serif on the top, hind legs form a descender serif, and forelegs form the remaining serif. Here, the half-uncial is predominant, with the upper serif extended into hindquarters, the lower serif a lion's head. Overleaf, fig. 69 b is similarly constructed.

Fig. 69

Lappet from lion's crown

ends in a grape bunch. Its tail tassel sprouts three banded lobes.

a

This lion has hardly any knots, in contrast to this lion and bird below.

b

c

Fíg. 70

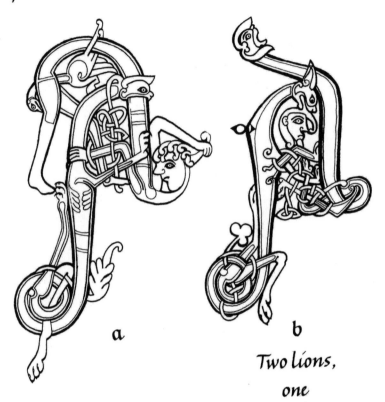

a

Lion, man and bird.

b

Two lions,
one
tête-coupée
or
decapitated head
motif.

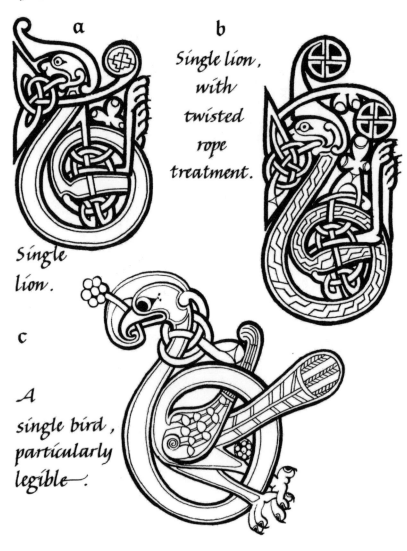

a

Single
lion.

b

Single lion,
with
twisted
rope
treatment.

c

A
single bird,
particularly
legible.

FIg. 72

Lion with tongue-and-forelock knot.

Lion with topknot ending in single spiral.

Lion with topknot ending in trilobe tassel.

a

b

c

Fig. 73

In fig. 71 a,b we have seen two letters with lion heads corresponding to ascender serifs, and hind legs as terminals. These animals are incomplete. lacking forelegs! In fig. 72, we have the complete animal, as may be seen by turning the figure sideways. See how they run!

This lion's tail ends in a grape cluster.

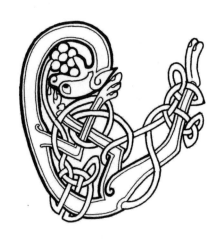

Fig. 74

You may have noticed that in the previous two chapters there were no birds, apart from one example in fig. 56 b. Likewise, in the animal alphabet, the bird assumes a secondary role, except for this one and its match, fig. 71 c. The bird is not as versatile as the quadruped, perhaps, but works well in a single serif letter here. It also might be applied to I, J, L, P, Q, U, V.

[429]

F͡g. 75

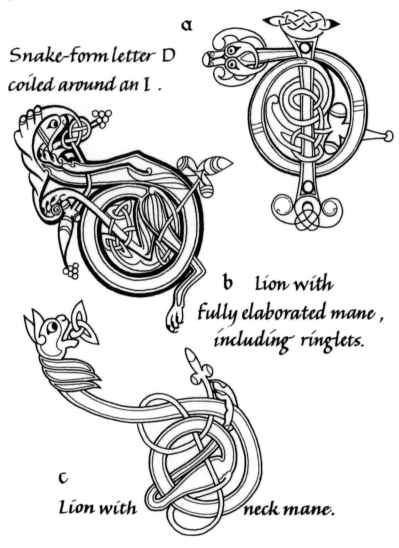

a

Snake-form letter D
coiled around an I .

b Lion with
fully elaborated mane ,
including ringlets.

c
Lion with   neck mane.

Fig.76

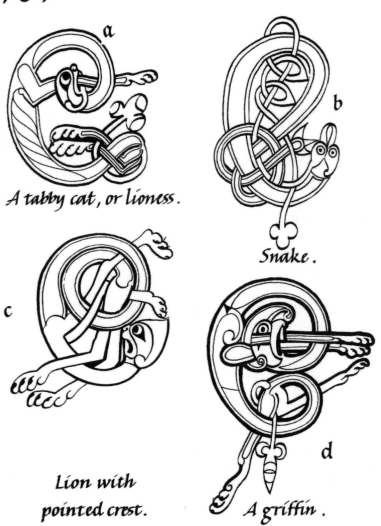

a

A tabby cat, or lioness.

b

Snake.

c

Lion with
pointed crest.

d

A griffin.

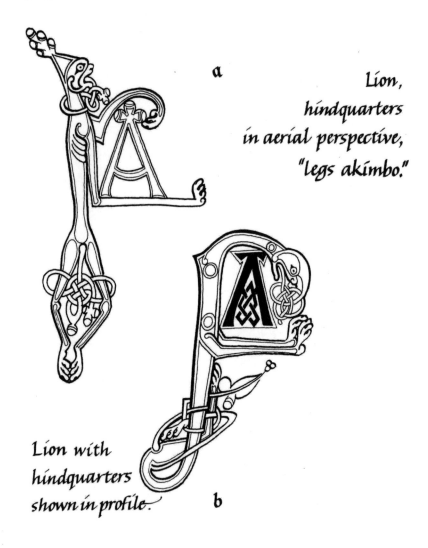

a

Lion,
hindquarters
in aerial perspective,
"legs akimbo."

Lion with
hindquarters
shown in profile.   b

a

Lion with paw
extended
in the air.

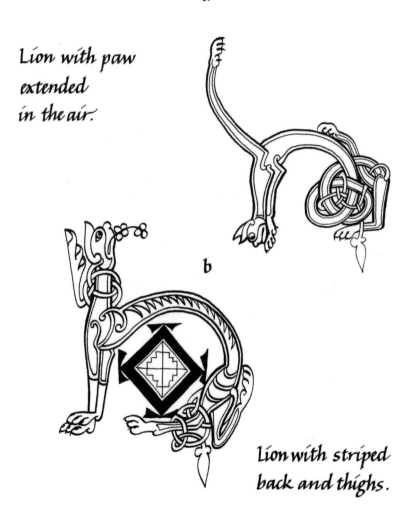

b

Lion with striped
back and thighs.

Lion rampant , a basic ascender.

Lion with crescentic ears, shoulder mane pattern
and crescent ribs.

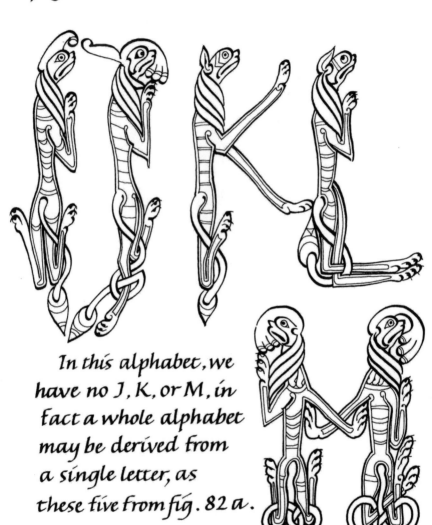

In this alphabet, we
have no J, K, or M, in
fact a whole alphabet
may be derived from
a single letter, as
these five from fig. 82 a.

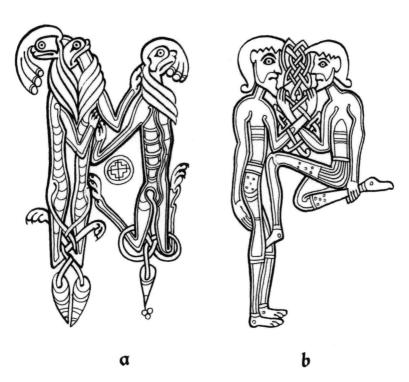

a   b

Three líons
with scrolled manes
and
ribbed flanks.   Two men.

Two lions with split ribbon necks and waists tied
in Josephine knots.

Two lions.

Fig.85

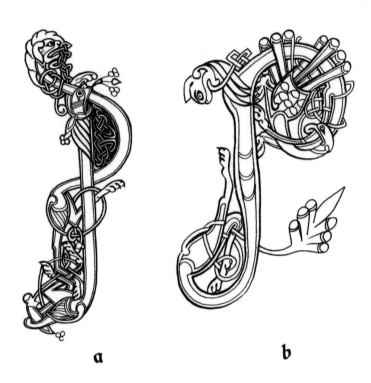

a   b

Two lions.
The descender could
double as a J.

Lion and bird.
Lion's tail has ringlets.

[440]

Fig.86

a   b

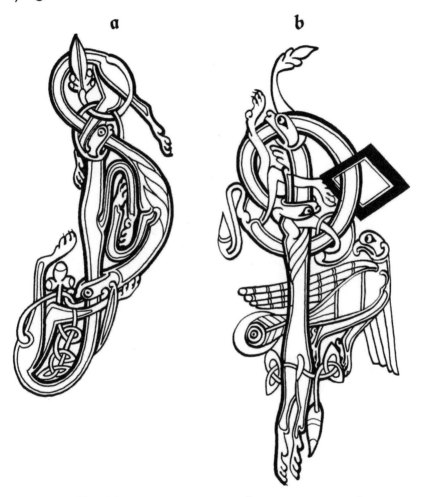

Two lions.   Two lions and an eagle.

Fig. 87

This letter has a serrated edge, and also an
unusual curl for a serif.

Fig.88

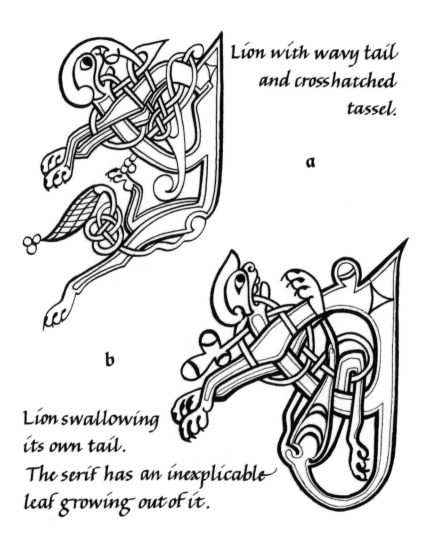

Lion with wavy tail
and crosshatched
tassel.

a

b

Lion swallowing
its own tail.
The serif has an inexplicable
leaf growing out of it.

Fig. 89

Opposite :

a   Human figure with single leg.
b   Human figure with beard-and-tongue knot.

Below :

Two lionesses and bird. The hooped cat has the
cheek bars that signify whiskers.

Fíg. 90

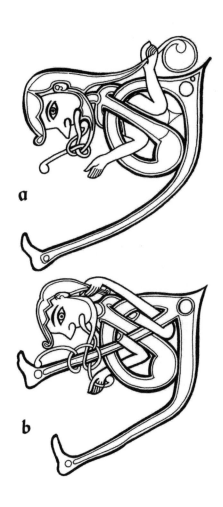

a

b

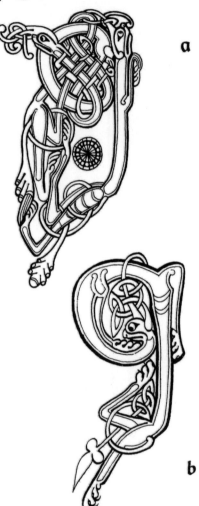

a

Two lions.
Separated,
they make a C and J.

Lion.

b

Lion with full-maned lion head serif.

Fig.93   Monogram 51.

Two lions.
The lion of the I has a trilobe mane.

[448]

Lion suffocating a bird.

Fig. 95

Lion with trefoil tail,

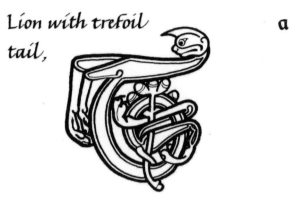

a

Lion with trefoil tail adapted to a monogram.

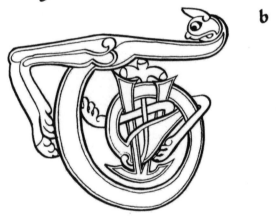

b

Fig.96   Monogram TU.

Lion suffocating a bird.

a

Lion with triangular extension on the curve.

b

Fig. 97

Two lionesses.

Fïʒ. 98

Two serpents with manes.

[453]

Fig. 99

Opposed lions with tongues tied in a knot.

※

ANIMAL AMPERSANDS

MATCHING SET of amper –
sands, belonging with the
previous alphabet, filled
with snakes and birds, displays the ver-
satility of this form of lettering, here
verging on the boundary between charac-
ter and decoration. In fact, these designs
are sometimes mistaken for ornaments
in themselves, taken out of context and
used as part of a border, or as jewelry
motifs. Enlarged, they make good de-
cals also.

Fig.100

One snake.

MOST OF THESE ANIMAL AMPersands take the form of the so-called snake of Celtic art. It was a latecomer to the repertory of ornament, a speciality of the Book of Kells, or one of the artists of that Book. Even in the kells animal alphabet, the snake is not much used, compared to the lion and the eagle. Exceptions are *figs 75a, 76b, 98.*

fig.101

Two snakes biting.

IN THE ALPHABET of DECORATED letters,
chapter III, there are no snakes either,
but in chapter IV it occurs in fig. 62 b.
There it appears in a very simple form.
The form is quite definite, though: the
head is shown from above, the eyes set in
two touching lobes which may be drawn
out into freehand knots; a third lobe
provides the creature with a bill or snout

[457]

fig. 102

Two snakes and a fish.

that may be treated in a variety of
ways; and the creature's body ends in a
tail, also amenable to variation. In
fig. 102, the tails are fishy crescents, one
tipped with little balls, the other joined
to its owners snout, as if being chewed.
Except the tail is not that of the nibbler.
It belongs to the head with its tongue
licking out across its flexed gill lappet.

fig.103

Two snakes.

IN *fig.*103, each snake may be read as one of the letters *et*. The former has its right ear bent sharply under its throat. It bites on the other ear, also sharply bent, but forward; the latter has ear lappets crossing its neck. Both have an ear terminating in a foliate tassel, similar to the lion's tail of *fig.*104. Here the bird's crest curves forward and

Fıᵹ.104

palmates in three lobes such as used for the ringlets of the lions' forelocks, as in *fig.82*. The treatment of lion mane

Lion biting bird?

and bird crest is carried over to the treatment of the snake's head and tail fin lappet, suggesting further such adaptations to an as yet unrealised snake alphabet. Compare the ears of *figs* 101

Fïg.105

and 75 ; or snout and tail fin of fig.105
with that of fig. 76 b.

Two snakes.

Fig. 76 b has a teardrop on its nose, like
fig.105 . Both have triplex tails , the
former a crescent-and-spike; the latter,
however is a further development, intro-

[461]

ducing the cat's-paw motif of fig. 15 as
an alternative tail fin for the snake. In
fig. 105 the snake's topknot is fully devel-

Single snake with fishtail.

oped fore-and-aft, like the mane of fig. 75 b.
In figs 103-107 the snakes have borrowed a
shoulder bulge from a lion as at fig.104.
Finally, the mane treatment of fig. 78 b,
with its toenailed lobes, as well as the

fig. 107

trefoil tail tassels of *fig. 75b* come together in the gill-lappets of *fig . 107,* one
of which has a secondary ringlet lobe.

Twoheaded snake.

These leonine ringlets and tassels, so like
foliage, are the basis of the Irish Urnes
style of the dawning Viking age. They
were the Animal Style master's swan
song: the fourth and final part of the
Book of Kells lacks his astounding legacy.

[463]

Fig. 108   Set of riveted ampersands.

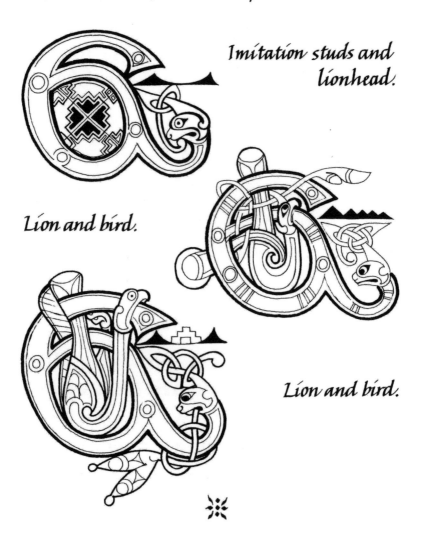

Imitation studs and
lionhead.

Lion and bird.

Lion and bird.

ANGULAR CAPITALS

NE OF THE LEAST KNOWN yet most excitingly malleable Celtic scripts, these decorative capitals were created as a display alphabet by the illuminators of the mid-seventh century Columban or Irish scriptoria. They no doubt felt the need to have a third type of script to make up for the birth of minuscule script – equivalent to our modern lower case lettering – as an alternative to majuscule, half uncial, which hitherto served as text as well as display script.

[465]

Fig. 109 Angular alphabet.

Fig. 110   Beginning of Luke, Lichfield.

Lichfield Gospel Book, folio 221. Luke 1:1.
quidem multi conati sunt ordinare...

[467]

FIG. 111   Beginning of Matthew, Lindisfarne.

Lindisfarne, folio 27. Math. 1:1. (*Liber*) *gene-rationis IHU XPI, filii David, filii Abraham.*

[468]

Lindisfarne , folio 95.
Mark 1 : 1, 2.
Initium evangelii
I·H·U X·P·I filii dei.
Sicut scribtum est..

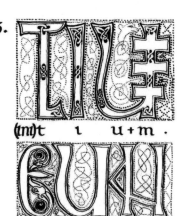

(in)t   i   u + m .

e   v   a + n -

g   e   l   i   I H U ·

x   p   i · f i l i · D · i · s i c u t ·

s c r i b t u m · e s t †

FIG. 113   Beginning of Luke, Lindisfarne.

Lindisfarne, fol. 139.
folio 139. Luke 1:1.
(Q) uoniam quidem
multi conati sunt
ordinare narrationem
Forasmuch as many
have taken in hand to
set forth a declaration.

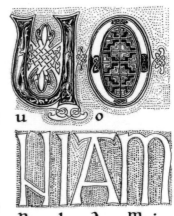

Fig .114   Beginning of John, Lindisfarne.

r i n   ci p   i o

e r a t   v e r b u m

&   v e r b u m   e r a t

a p u d   D(omini)m & D(eu) s

The Book of Lindisfarne, folio 211;
beginning of the Gospel of St John:
(In p) rincipio erat verbum et verbum erat apud
dominum et deus (erat verbum)

The smaller letters are 8-10 nibwidths high.

Fig. 115 Angular knotwork letters, Kells.

**KELLS
FOLIO 183 R**

(E) rat autem hora tercia

Mark 15:25

(e) r a t .

a u t + e m .

h + o r a : t e r cia·

FIG. 116   Angular outlined letters, Kells.

KELLS FOLIO 124 R

u   n   c · c   r   u

(T) unc cru-cifixerunt XPI cum eo duos latrones
Matt. 27:38

Fig. 117

**KELLS
FOLIO 292 R**

(In princi) pio erat verbum verum.

John 1 : 1

Fig. 118   Interspace filling

**KELLS
FOLIO 285R**

Autem sabbati valde de lu(culo).   Luke 26:1

KELLS FOLIO 29R stacked title block.

[*Liber*]
generationis

[475]

KELLS
FOLIO
8R

XPIINBETRLEHI Ju

x p l · i n b e t h l e m . Ju-

DEAEMATI

d e a e . M a g i ·

HUNERAOFFERUNT B

m u n e r a · o f f e r u n t &

INFANTESINTER

i n f a n t e s · i n t e r ~

FICIUNTUR RETRESSID

f i c i u n t u r · r e g r e s s i o .

THE·QUICK·BROWN·FOX·JUMPS·OVER·THE·LAZY·DOG

DETAIL of decorative border, folio 285 R

Glossary of terms

DECAL. A design transferred onto the back of a jacket.

FYLFOT. The Saxon term for swastika.

KEY PATTERN. Celtic fret pattern : diagonal, interlocking angular paths resembling L-shaped slots cut in keys. See Beginners' Manual, Ch.II.

LAPPET. Literally, a loose, hanging part of something ; a secondary ribbon or knot extending from a main figure in an animal pattern, as an ear, tongue or tail.

LENTOID. Shaped like a lens, or lentil.

MEROVINGIAN. The first Frankish dynasty , c. 500 - 750 .

PELTA. Term for a classic motif that is derived from the form of a palm leaf, shaped like a fan, the outer corners of which may be elaborated into spirals.

a   b   c

SALTIRE. *Diagonal cross.*
STEP PATTERN. *Straight lines bent like the steps of a stair; see Beginner's Manual.*
TRIQUETRA. *Simple triangular knot with a continuous path, very simple and fun to do, which is what makes it the most popular Celtic knot to this day. It may be constructed by the scribe's method in two ways, open or closed form.*

See Appendix to Knotwork for 60 triquetras.
Open form:

Closed form:

Split-ribbon form:

TRISKELE. *A spiral whirligig with three arms; also spelt 'triskel'.*

Triskele:

[479]

Appendix

Recommended List of Books to Read

Janet Backhouse,
The Lindisfarne Gospels, Oxford 1981

Françoise Henry,
Irish Art, London 1970
--- *The Book of Kells*, London 1974

Aidan Meehan,
Celtic Design: A Beginner's Manual,
London 1991
--- *Celtic Design: Knotwork*, London 1991
--- *Celtic Design: Animal Patterns*,
London 1992

Carl Nordenfalk,
Celtic and Anglo-Saxon Painting
London 1977